TEACHER'S PET PUBLICATIONS

PUZZLE PACK
for
A Doll's House
based on the play by
Henrik Ibsen

Written by
William T. Collins

© 2005 Teacher's Pet Publications
All Rights Reserved

The materials in this packet are copyrighted
by Teacher's Pet Publications, Inc.

These pages may be duplicated by the purchaser
for use in the purchaser's own classroom.

Copying any of these materials and distributing them
for any other purpose is a violation of the copyright laws.

© 2005 Teacher's Pet Publications, Inc.
www.tpet.com

INTRODUCTION
If you already own the LitPlan for this title, this Puzzle Pack will refresh your Unit Resource Materials and Vocabulary Resource Materials sections plus give you additional materials you can substitute into the tests. If you do not already have a complete LitPlan, these pages will give you some supplemental materials to use with your own plan. There are two main groups of materials: one set for unit words (such as characters' names, symbols, places, etc.) and one set for vocabulary words associated with the book.

WORD LIST
There is a word list for both the unit words and the vocabulary words. These lists show you which words are being used in the materials and the clues or definitions being used for those words. You may want to give students a word list with clues/definitions to help them, or you may want students to only have a word list (without clues/definitions) if you want them to work a little harder. Both are available for duplication. The word lists can also be your "calling key" for the bingo games.

FILL IN THE BLANK AND MATCHING
There are 4 each of the fill in the blank and matching worksheets for both the unit and vocabulary words. These pages can be used either as extra worksheets for students or as objective parts of a unit test. They can be done individually if students need extra help or as a whole class activity to review the material covered.

MAGIC SQUARES
The magic squares not only reinforce the material covered but also work on reasoning and math skills. Many teachers have told us that their students really enjoy doing these!

WORD SEARCH PUZZLES
The word search words go in all directions, as indicated on your answer keys. Two of the word search puzzles have the clues listed rather than the words. This makes the puzzle a little more difficult, but it reinforces the material better. Two word search puzzles have words only for students who find the clue puzzles too difficult.

CROSSWORD PUZZLES
Both unit and vocabulary word sections have 4 crossword puzzles.

BINGO CARDS
There are 32 individual bingo cards for the unit words and 32 individual bingo cards for the vocabulary words. You can use your word list as a "call list," calling the words at random and marking them off of your list as you go, or you could use the flash cards by cutting them apart and drawing the words at random from a hat (or box or whatever). To make a better review, you might ask for the definition and spelling of each word as you call it out–or you could call out the definitions and have students tell you the words they need to look for on the puzzle.

JUGGLE LETTERS
The vocabulary juggle letter game is intended to help students learn the spellings of the words. One sheet has the definitions listed on it as an extra help for students who need it or to reinforce the definitions if you choose to do so.

FLASH CARDS
We've included a set of vocabulary flash cards you can duplicate, cut, and fold for your students. Some teachers make a few sets for general use by the class; others make a set for each student. Some teachers duplicate them for each student and have the students cut & fold their own. You can cut out just the words and put them in a hat, have each student pick out one word and write the definition and a sentence for that word. Students then swap words and papers, with the next student adding a sentence of his own under the last one. You can have students swap as many times as you like. Each time the student will read the sentences written prior to his own and then add a sentence. You can cut out the words and definitions separately and play "I Have; Who Has?" Each student in the room draws a word and definition. The first student says, "I have (the name of the word). Who has the definition?" The student with the definition reads it then says, "I have (the name of the vocabulary word she has). Who has the definition?" The round continues until all words and definitions have been given.

A Doll's House Word List

No.	Word	Clue/Definition
1.	ACT	Play division
2.	APPEARANCES	Nora realized Helmer was more concerned with this than with her
3.	BANK	Helmer was to get a promotion to manager of the _____ right after New Years
4.	BLACKMAIL	Krogstad wrote a letter to _____ Helmer
5.	CHILDREN	Nora didn't want to see hers at the end of Act One
6.	COPYING	Extra work Nora took on to help pay off the loan
7.	DOLL	A _____'s House
8.	FORGED	Nora _____ her father's signature on the note
9.	HAPPINESS	From now on _____ doesn't matter; all that matters is...the appearance
10.	HELMER	Nora's husband
11.	HOPE	Mrs. Linde gave Krogstad _____ for the future
12.	IBSEN	Author
13.	ITALY	Country where Torvald went to recover
14.	JUSTICE	And then to suffer this way for somebody else's sins. Is there any _____ in that?
15.	KROGSTAD	Lawyer from whom Nora borrowed money
16.	LARK	What's become of the little _____?
17.	LAWS	They don't inquire into motives
18.	LETTER	Krogstad wrote one to blackmail Helmer into letting him keep his job
19.	LINDE	Old friend of Nora; hopes to get a job at the bank
20.	LOAN	Nora got one from Krogstad
21.	LOVE	Dr. Rank declared his _____ for Nora
22.	MORAL	His _____ failings I could maybe overlook if I had to
23.	MOTHER	Most everyone who goes bad early in life had a _____ who's a chronic liar
24.	NORA	She borrowed money from Krogstad
25.	PAPA	I've been wronged greatly, Torvald--first by _____ and then by you.
26.	PEOPLE	And you're not even thinking what _____ will say
27.	PROMOTION	Helmer was expecting one at the beginning of the new year
28.	RANK	Doctor who has a terminal disease
29.	SCENE	Act division
30.	STAGE	Place where a play is put on
31.	SUICIDE	At the end of Act Two Nora decided to commit it
32.	THIN	Does your husband's love for you run so _____?
33.	TORVALD	Nora borrowed money to finance a trip to Italy for him

A Doll's House Fill In The Blanks 1

_____
_____
_____
_____
_____
_____
_____
_____
_____
_____
_____
_____
_____
_____
_____
_____
_____
_____
_____
_____

1. Does your husband's love for you run so ____?
2. Extra work Nora took on to help pay off the loan
3. Country where Torvald went to recover
4. She borrowed money from Krogstad
5. Nora got one from Krogstad
6. Nora's husband
7. Doctor who has a terminal disease
8. Helmer was expecting one at the beginning of the new year
9. And then to suffer this way for somebody else's sins. Is there any ____ in that?
10. What's become of the little ____?
11. They don't inquire into motives
12. Most everyone who goes bad early in life had a ____ who's a chronic liar
13. Nora borrowed money to finance a trip to Italy for him
14. Krogstad wrote one to blackmail Helmer into letting him keep his job
15. Play division
16. Lawyer from whom Nora borrowed money
17. Dr. Rank declared his ____ for Nora
18. Helmer was to get a promotion to manager of the _____ right after New Years
19. From now on ____ doesn't matter; all that matters is...the appearance
20. His ____ failings I could maybe overlook if I had to

A Doll's House Fill In The Blanks 1 Answer Key

THIN	1. Does your husband's love for you run so ____?
COPYING	2. Extra work Nora took on to help pay off the loan
ITALY	3. Country where Torvald went to recover
NORA	4. She borrowed money from Krogstad
LOAN	5. Nora got one from Krogstad
HELMER	6. Nora's husband
RANK	7. Doctor who has a terminal disease
PROMOTION	8. Helmer was expecting one at the beginning of the new year
JUSTICE	9. And then to suffer this way for somebody else's sins. Is there any ____ in that?
LARK	10. What's become of the little ____?
LAWS	11. They don't inquire into motives
MOTHER	12. Most everyone who goes bad early in life had a ____ who's a chronic liar
TORVALD	13. Nora borrowed money to finance a trip to Italy for him
LETTER	14. Krogstad wrote one to blackmail Helmer into letting him keep his job
ACT	15. Play division
KROGSTAD	16. Lawyer from whom Nora borrowed money
LOVE	17. Dr. Rank declared his ____ for Nora
BANK	18. Helmer was to get a promotion to manager of the _____ right after New Years
HAPPINESS	19. From now on ____ doesn't matter; all that matters is...the appearance
MORAL	20. His ____ failings I could maybe overlook if I had to

A Doll's House Fill In The Blanks 2

_____
_____
_____
_____
_____
_____
_____
_____
_____
_____
_____
_____
_____
_____
_____
_____
_____
_____
_____
_____

1. Act division
2. Nora didn't want to see hers at the end of Act One
3. What's become of the little ____?
4. Nora ____ her father's signature on the note
5. Old friend of Nora; hopes to get a job at the bank
6. Dr. Rank declared his ____ for Nora
7. Nora got one from Krogstad
8. Lawyer from whom Nora borrowed money
9. I've been wronged greatly, Torvald--first by ____ and then by you.
10. Place where a play is put on
11. Most everyone who goes bad early in life had a ____ who's a chronic liar
12. They don't inquire into motives
13. Nora realized Helmer was more concerned with this than with her
14. Helmer was expecting one at the beginning of the new year
15. Krogstad wrote a letter to ____ Helmer
16. Does your husband's love for you run so ____?
17. Doctor who has a terminal disease
18. At the end of Act Two Nora decided to commit it
19. Krogstad wrote one to blackmail Helmer into letting him keep his job
20. Author

A Doll's House Fill In The Blanks 2 Answer Key

SCENE	1. Act division
CHILDREN	2. Nora didn't want to see hers at the end of Act One
LARK	3. What's become of the little ____?
FORGED	4. Nora ____ her father's signature on the note
LINDE	5. Old friend of Nora; hopes to get a job at the bank
LOVE	6. Dr. Rank declared his ____ for Nora
LOAN	7. Nora got one from Krogstad
KROGSTAD	8. Lawyer from whom Nora borrowed money
PAPA	9. I've been wronged greatly, Torvald--first by ____ and then by you.
STAGE	10. Place where a play is put on
MOTHER	11. Most everyone who goes bad early in life had a ____ who's a chronic liar
LAWS	12. They don't inquire into motives
APPEARANCES	13. Nora realized Helmer was more concerned with this than with her
PROMOTION	14. Helmer was expecting one at the beginning of the new year
BLACKMAIL	15. Krogstad wrote a letter to ____ Helmer
THIN	16. Does your husband's love for you run so ____?
RANK	17. Doctor who has a terminal disease
SUICIDE	18. At the end of Act Two Nora decided to commit it
LETTER	19. Krogstad wrote one to blackmail Helmer into letting him keep his job
IBSEN	20. Author

A Doll's House Fill In The Blanks 3

_____

_____

_____

_____

_____

_____

_____

_____

_____

_____

_____

_____

_____

_____

_____

_____

_____

_____

_____

_____

1. Author
2. I've been wronged greatly, Torvald--first by _____ and then by you.
3. Nora didn't want to see hers at the end of Act One
4. Nora _____ her father's signature on the note
5. She borrowed money from Krogstad
6. Mrs. Linde gave Krogstad _____ for the future
7. Lawyer from whom Nora borrowed money
8. And then to suffer this way for somebody else's sins. Is there any _____ in that?
9. Dr. Rank declared his _____ for Nora
10. Nora borrowed money to finance a trip to Italy for him
11. Country where Torvald went to recover
12. Play division
13. From now on _____ doesn't matter; all that matters is...the appearance
14. At the end of Act Two Nora decided to commit it
15. Act division
16. Old friend of Nora; hopes to get a job at the bank
17. Helmer was to get a promotion to manager of the _____ right after New Years
18. Nora realized Helmer was more concerned with this than with her
19. Krogstad wrote one to blackmail Helmer into letting him keep his job
20. Place where a play is put on

A Doll's House Fill In The Blanks 3 Answer Key

IBSEN	1. Author
PAPA	2. I've been wronged greatly, Torvald--first by ____ and then by you.
CHILDREN	3. Nora didn't want to see hers at the end of Act One
FORGED	4. Nora ____ her father's signature on the note
NORA	5. She borrowed money from Krogstad
HOPE	6. Mrs. Linde gave Krogstad ____ for the future
KROGSTAD	7. Lawyer from whom Nora borrowed money
JUSTICE	8. And then to suffer this way for somebody else's sins. Is there any ____ in that?
LOVE	9. Dr. Rank declared his ____ for Nora
TORVALD	10. Nora borrowed money to finance a trip to Italy for him
ITALY	11. Country where Torvald went to recover
ACT	12. Play division
HAPPINESS	13. From now on ____ doesn't matter; all that matters is...the appearance
SUICIDE	14. At the end of Act Two Nora decided to commit it
SCENE	15. Act division
LINDE	16. Old friend of Nora; hopes to get a job at the bank
BANK	17. Helmer was to get a promotion to manager of the ____ right after New Years
APPEARANCES	18. Nora realized Helmer was more concerned with this than with her
LETTER	19. Krogstad wrote one to blackmail Helmer into letting him keep his job
STAGE	20. Place where a play is put on

A Doll's House Fill In The Blanks 4

_____

_____

_____

_____

_____

_____

_____

_____

_____

_____

_____

_____

_____

_____

_____

_____

_____

_____

_____

_____

1. Nora realized Helmer was more concerned with this than with her
2. And then to suffer this way for somebody else's sins. Is there any _____ in that?
3. Helmer was expecting one at the beginning of the new year
4. Nora _____ her father's signature on the note
5. Nora borrowed money to finance a trip to Italy for him
6. Author
7. Play division
8. They don't inquire into motives
9. And you're not even thinking what _____ will say
10. From now on _____ doesn't matter; all that matters is...the appearance
11. Helmer was to get a promotion to manager of the _____ right after New Years
12. Lawyer from whom Nora borrowed money
13. Does your husband's love for you run so _____?
14. Nora's husband
15. She borrowed money from Krogstad
16. Country where Torvald went to recover
17. His _____ failings I could maybe overlook if I had to
18. Krogstad wrote one to blackmail Helmer into letting him keep his job
19. Nora didn't want to see hers at the end of Act One
20. I've been wronged greatly, Torvald--first by _____ and then by you.

A Doll's House Fill In The Blanks 4 Answer Key

APPEARANCES	1. Nora realized Helmer was more concerned with this than with her
JUSTICE	2. And then to suffer this way for somebody else's sins. Is there any ____ in that?
PROMOTION	3. Helmer was expecting one at the beginning of the new year
FORGED	4. Nora ____ her father's signature on the note
TORVALD	5. Nora borrowed money to finance a trip to Italy for him
IBSEN	6. Author
ACT	7. Play division
LAWS	8. They don't inquire into motives
PEOPLE	9. And you're not even thinking what ____ will say
HAPPINESS	10. From now on ____ doesn't matter; all that matters is...the appearance
BANK	11. Helmer was to get a promotion to manager of the _____ right after New Years
KROGSTAD	12. Lawyer from whom Nora borrowed money
THIN	13. Does your husband's love for you run so ____?
HELMER	14. Nora's husband
NORA	15. She borrowed money from Krogstad
ITALY	16. Country where Torvald went to recover
MORAL	17. His ____ failings I could maybe overlook if I had to
LETTER	18. Krogstad wrote one to blackmail Helmer into letting him keep his job
CHILDREN	19. Nora didn't want to see hers at the end of Act One
PAPA	20. I've been wronged greatly, Torvald—first by ____ and then by you.

A Doll's House Matching 1

___ 1. CHILDREN
___ 2. ACT
___ 3. NORA
___ 4. LINDE
___ 5. DOLL
___ 6. IBSEN
___ 7. LOVE
___ 8. MOTHER
___ 9. MORAL
___10. LETTER
___11. HAPPINESS
___12. RANK
___13. JUSTICE
___14. BLACKMAIL
___15. PROMOTION
___16. FORGED
___17. HELMER
___18. COPYING
___19. SUICIDE
___20. STAGE
___21. KROGSTAD
___22. ITALY
___23. SCENE
___24. APPEARANCES
___25. LARK

A. And then to suffer this way for somebody else's sins. Is there any ____ in that?
B. Old friend of Nora; hopes to get a job at the bank
C. Most everyone who goes bad early in life had a ____ who's a chronic liar
D. Nora ____ her father's signature on the note
E. Nora didn't want to see hers at the end of Act One
F. Country where Torvald went to recover
G. She borrowed money from Krogstad
H. A ____'s House
I. Author
J. Play division
K. Act division
L. Place where a play is put on
M. Extra work Nora took on to help pay off the loan
N. What's become of the little ____?
O. At the end of Act Two Nora decided to commit it
P. Helmer was expecting one at the beginning of the new year
Q. Krogstad wrote a letter to ____ Helmer
R. Dr. Rank declared his ____ for Nora
S. Lawyer from whom Nora borrowed money
T. Nora's husband
U. Doctor who has a terminal disease
V. From now on ____ doesn't matter; all that matters is...the appearance
W. Nora realized Helmer was more concerned with this than with her
X. His ____ failings I could maybe overlook if I had to
Y. Krogstad wrote one to blackmail Helmer into letting him keep his job

A Doll's House Matching 1 Answer Key

E - 1. CHILDREN
J - 2. ACT
G - 3. NORA
B - 4. LINDE
H - 5. DOLL
I - 6. IBSEN
R - 7. LOVE
C - 8. MOTHER
X - 9. MORAL
Y - 10. LETTER
V - 11. HAPPINESS
U - 12. RANK
A - 13. JUSTICE
Q - 14. BLACKMAIL
P - 15. PROMOTION
D - 16. FORGED
T - 17. HELMER
M - 18. COPYING
O - 19. SUICIDE
L - 20. STAGE
S - 21. KROGSTAD
F - 22. ITALY
K - 23. SCENE
W - 24. APPEARANCES
N - 25. LARK

A. And then to suffer this way for somebody else's sins. Is there any ____ in that?
B. Old friend of Nora; hopes to get a job at the bank
C. Most everyone who goes bad early in life had a ____ who's a chronic liar
D. Nora ____ her father's signature on the note
E. Nora didn't want to see hers at the end of Act One
F. Country where Torvald went to recover
G. She borrowed money from Krogstad
H. A ____'s House
I. Author
J. Play division
K. Act division
L. Place where a play is put on
M. Extra work Nora took on to help pay off the loan
N. What's become of the little ____?
O. At the end of Act Two Nora decided to commit it
P. Helmer was expecting one at the beginning of the new year
Q. Krogstad wrote a letter to ____ Helmer
R. Dr. Rank declared his ____ for Nora
S. Lawyer from whom Nora borrowed money
T. Nora's husband
U. Doctor who has a terminal disease
V. From now on ____ doesn't matter; all that matters is...the appearance
W. Nora realized Helmer was more concerned with this than with her
X. His ____ failings I could maybe overlook if I had to
Y. Krogstad wrote one to blackmail Helmer into letting him keep his job

A Doll's House Matching 2

___ 1. LAWS
___ 2. STAGE
___ 3. SCENE
___ 4. PAPA
___ 5. JUSTICE
___ 6. APPEARANCES
___ 7. PROMOTION
___ 8. RANK
___ 9. LINDE
___ 10. TORVALD
___ 11. HOPE
___ 12. HELMER
___ 13. SUICIDE
___ 14. BLACKMAIL
___ 15. LETTER
___ 16. DOLL
___ 17. COPYING
___ 18. LARK
___ 19. LOVE
___ 20. CHILDREN
___ 21. BANK
___ 22. ITALY
___ 23. ACT
___ 24. LOAN
___ 25. MOTHER

A. Helmer was expecting one at the beginning of the new year
B. Act division
C. Dr. Rank declared his ____ for Nora
D. Nora didn't want to see hers at the end of Act One
E. Extra work Nora took on to help pay off the loan
F. Doctor who has a terminal disease
G. Most everyone who goes bad early in life had a ____ who's a chronic liar
H. Nora got one from Krogstad
I. Mrs. Linde gave Krogstad ____ for the future
J. Place where a play is put on
K. I've been wronged greatly, Torvald--first by ____ and then by you.
L. Country where Torvald went to recover
M. Krogstad wrote a letter to ____ Helmer
N. Play division
O. Nora borrowed money to finance a trip to Italy for him
P. What's become of the little ____?
Q. At the end of Act Two Nora decided to commit it
R. Nora's husband
S. Nora realized Helmer was more concerned with this than with her
T. Krogstad wrote one to blackmail Helmer into letting him keep his job
U. A ____'s House
V. They don't inquire into motives
W. And then to suffer this way for somebody else's sins. Is there any ____ in that?
X. Helmer was to get a promotion to manager of the ____ right after New Years
Y. Old friend of Nora; hopes to get a job at the bank

A Doll's House Matching 2 Answer Key

V - 1. LAWS	A. Helmer was expecting one at the beginning of the new year
J - 2. STAGE	B. Act division
B - 3. SCENE	C. Dr. Rank declared his ____ for Nora
K - 4. PAPA	D. Nora didn't want to see hers at the end of Act One
W - 5. JUSTICE	E. Extra work Nora took on to help pay off the loan
S - 6. APPEARANCES	F. Doctor who has a terminal disease
A - 7. PROMOTION	G. Most everyone who goes bad early in life had a ____ who's a chronic liar
F - 8. RANK	H. Nora got one from Krogstad
Y - 9. LINDE	I. Mrs. Linde gave Krogstad ____ for the future
O -10. TORVALD	J. Place where a play is put on
I - 11. HOPE	K. I've been wronged greatly, Torvald--first by ____ and then by you.
R -12. HELMER	L. Country where Torvald went to recover
Q -13. SUICIDE	M. Krogstad wrote a letter to ____ Helmer
M -14. BLACKMAIL	N. Play division
T -15. LETTER	O. Nora borrowed money to finance a trip to Italy for him
U -16. DOLL	P. What's become of the little ____?
E -17. COPYING	Q. At the end of Act Two Nora decided to commit it
P -18. LARK	R. Nora's husband
C -19. LOVE	S. Nora realized Helmer was more concerned with this than with her
D -20. CHILDREN	T. Krogstad wrote one to blackmail Helmer into letting him keep his job
X -21. BANK	U. A ____'s House
L -22. ITALY	V. They don't inquire into motives
N -23. ACT	W. And then to suffer this way for somebody else's sins. Is there any ____ in that?
H -24. LOAN	X. Helmer was to get a promotion to manager of the ____ right after New Years
G -25. MOTHER	Y. Old friend of Nora; hopes to get a job at the bank

Copyrighted

A Doll's House Matching 3

___ 1. ACT
___ 2. LETTER
___ 3. IBSEN
___ 4. CHILDREN
___ 5. FORGED
___ 6. LOVE
___ 7. LOAN
___ 8. SUICIDE
___ 9. LAWS
___ 10. MOTHER
___ 11. HAPPINESS
___ 12. JUSTICE
___ 13. TORVALD
___ 14. HELMER
___ 15. MORAL
___ 16. KROGSTAD
___ 17. BLACKMAIL
___ 18. RANK
___ 19. STAGE
___ 20. APPEARANCES
___ 21. THIN
___ 22. LARK
___ 23. LINDE
___ 24. PEOPLE
___ 25. PROMOTION

A. Author
B. Doctor who has a terminal disease
C. Krogstad wrote a letter to ____ Helmer
D. Nora's husband
E. Nora got one from Krogstad
F. Most everyone who goes bad early in life had a ____ who's a chronic liar
G. Nora borrowed money to finance a trip to Italy for him
H. Nora didn't want to see hers at the end of Act One
I. From now on ____ doesn't matter; all that matters is...the appearance
J. His ____ failings I could maybe overlook if I had to
K. Krogstad wrote one to blackmail Helmer into letting him keep his job
L. Helmer was expecting one at the beginning of the new year
M. Dr. Rank declared his ____ for Nora
N. Nora ____ her father's signature on the note
O. Nora realized Helmer was more concerned with this than with her
P. At the end of Act Two Nora decided to commit it
Q. Place where a play is put on
R. Old friend of Nora; hopes to get a job at the bank
S. They don't inquire into motives
T. Play division
U. Lawyer from whom Nora borrowed money
V. Does your husband's love for you run so ____?
W. What's become of the little ____?
X. And then to suffer this way for somebody else's sins. Is there any ____ in that?
Y. And you're not even thinking what ____ will say

A Doll's House Matching 3 Answer Key

T - 1. ACT
K - 2. LETTER
A - 3. IBSEN
H - 4. CHILDREN
N - 5. FORGED
M - 6. LOVE
E - 7. LOAN
P - 8. SUICIDE
S - 9. LAWS
F - 10. MOTHER
I - 11. HAPPINESS
X - 12. JUSTICE
G - 13. TORVALD
D - 14. HELMER
J - 15. MORAL
U - 16. KROGSTAD
C - 17. BLACKMAIL
B - 18. RANK
Q - 19. STAGE
O - 20. APPEARANCES
V - 21. THIN
W - 22. LARK
R - 23. LINDE
Y - 24. PEOPLE
L - 25. PROMOTION

A. Author
B. Doctor who has a terminal disease
C. Krogstad wrote a letter to ____ Helmer
D. Nora's husband
E. Nora got one from Krogstad
F. Most everyone who goes bad early in life had a ____ who's a chronic liar
G. Nora borrowed money to finance a trip to Italy for him
H. Nora didn't want to see hers at the end of Act One
I. From now on ____ doesn't matter; all that matters is...the appearance
J. His ____ failings I could maybe overlook if I had to
K. Krogstad wrote one to blackmail Helmer into letting him keep his job
L. Helmer was expecting one at the beginning of the new year
M. Dr. Rank declared his ____ for Nora
N. Nora ____ her father's signature on the note
O. Nora realized Helmer was more concerned with this than with her
P. At the end of Act Two Nora decided to commit it
Q. Place where a play is put on
R. Old friend of Nora; hopes to get a job at the bank
S. They don't inquire into motives
T. Play division
U. Lawyer from whom Nora borrowed money
V. Does your husband's love for you run so ____?
W. What's become of the little ____?
X. And then to suffer this way for somebody else's sins. Is there any ____ in that?
Y. And you're not even thinking what ____ will say

A Doll's House Matching 4

___ 1. FORGED   A. Krogstad wrote a letter to ____ Helmer
___ 2. MORAL   B. At the end of Act Two Nora decided to commit it
___ 3. DOLL   C. And you're not even thinking what ____ will say
___ 4. ITALY   D. Nora's husband
___ 5. LOVE   E. Nora didn't want to see hers at the end of Act One
___ 6. APPEARANCES   F. Extra work Nora took on to help pay off the loan
___ 7. STAGE   G. Doctor who has a terminal disease
___ 8. BANK   H. Does your husband's love for you run so ____?
___ 9. JUSTICE   I. His ____ failings I could maybe overlook if I had to
___ 10. RANK   J. Old friend of Nora; hopes to get a job at the bank
___ 11. PEOPLE   K. They don't inquire into motives
___ 12. HAPPINESS   L. Helmer was expecting one at the beginning of the new year
___ 13. CHILDREN   M. Dr. Rank declared his ____ for Nora
___ 14. COPYING   N. Nora ____ her father's signature on the note
___ 15. NORA   O. Lawyer from whom Nora borrowed money
___ 16. SUICIDE   P. From now on ____ doesn't matter; all that matters is...the appearance
___ 17. BLACKMAIL   Q. Most everyone who goes bad early in life had a ____ who's a chronic liar
___ 18. PROMOTION   R. Play division
___ 19. LINDE   S. Place where a play is put on
___ 20. MOTHER   T. A ____'s House
___ 21. ACT   U. And then to suffer this way for somebody else's sins. Is there any ____ in that?
___ 22. HELMER   V. Nora realized Helmer was more concerned with this than with her
___ 23. THIN   W. Helmer was to get a promotion to manager of the ____ right after New Years
___ 24. KROGSTAD   X. Country where Torvald went to recover
___ 25. LAWS   Y. She borrowed money from Krogstad

A Doll's House Matching 4 Answer Key

N - 1. FORGED	A. Krogstad wrote a letter to ____ Helmer
I - 2. MORAL	B. At the end of Act Two Nora decided to commit it
T - 3. DOLL	C. And you're not even thinking what ____ will say
X - 4. ITALY	D. Nora's husband
M - 5. LOVE	E. Nora didn't want to see hers at the end of Act One
V - 6. APPEARANCES	F. Extra work Nora took on to help pay off the loan
S - 7. STAGE	G. Doctor who has a terminal disease
W - 8. BANK	H. Does your husband's love for you run so ____?
U - 9. JUSTICE	I. His ____ failings I could maybe overlook if I had to
G -10. RANK	J. Old friend of Nora; hopes to get a job at the bank
C -11. PEOPLE	K. They don't inquire into motives
P -12. HAPPINESS	L. Helmer was expecting one at the beginning of the new year
E -13. CHILDREN	M. Dr. Rank declared his ____ for Nora
F -14. COPYING	N. Nora ____ her father's signature on the note
Y -15. NORA	O. Lawyer from whom Nora borrowed money
B -16. SUICIDE	P. From now on ____ doesn't matter; all that matters is...the appearance
A -17. BLACKMAIL	Q. Most everyone who goes bad early in life had a ____ who's a chronic liar
L -18. PROMOTION	R. Play division
J -19. LINDE	S. Place where a play is put on
Q -20. MOTHER	T. A ____'s House
R -21. ACT	U. And then to suffer this way for somebody else's sins. Is there any ____ in that?
D -22. HELMER	V. Nora realized Helmer was more concerned with this than with her
H -23. THIN	W. Helmer was to get a promotion to manager of the ____ right after New Years
O -24. KROGSTAD	X. Country where Torvald went to recover
K -25. LAWS	Y. She borrowed money from Krogstad

A Doll's House Magic Squares 1

Match the definition with the vocabulary word. Put your answers in the magic squares below. When your answers are correct, all columns and rows will add to the same number.

A. NORA
B. BLACKMAIL
C. LARK
D. LETTER
E. THIN
F. LOAN
G. HOPE
H. JUSTICE
I. PAPA
J. KROGSTAD
K. BANK
L. FORGED
M. RANK
N. TORVALD
O. ACT
P. LAWS

1. Doctor who has a terminal disease
2. Nora got one from Krogstad
3. And then to suffer this way for somebody else's sins. Is there any ____ in that?
4. Play division
5. Nora ____ her father's signature on the note
6. What's become of the little ____?
7. She borrowed money from Krogstad
8. Lawyer from whom Nora borrowed money
9. Helmer was to get a promotion to manager of the ____ right after New Years
10. Krogstad wrote one to blackmail Helmer into letting him keep his job
11. Krogstad wrote a letter to ____ Helmer
12. I've been wronged greatly, Torvald--first by ____ and then by you.
13. Nora borrowed money to finance a trip to Italy for him
14. Does your husband's love for you run so ____?
15. Mrs. Linde gave Krogstad ____ for the future
16. They don't inquire into motives

A=	B=	C=	D=
E=	F=	G=	H=
I=	J=	K=	L=
M=	N=	O=	P=

A Doll's House Magic Squares 1 Answer Key

Match the definition with the vocabulary word. Put your answers in the magic squares below. When your answers are correct, all columns and rows will add to the same number.

A. NORA
B. BLACKMAIL
C. LARK
D. LETTER
E. THIN
F. LOAN
G. HOPE
H. JUSTICE
I. PAPA
J. KROGSTAD
K. BANK
L. FORGED
M. RANK
N. TORVALD
O. ACT
P. LAWS

1. Doctor who has a terminal disease
2. Nora got one from Krogstad
3. And then to suffer this way for somebody else's sins. Is there any ____ in that?
4. Play division
5. Nora ____ her father's signature on the note
6. What's become of the little ____?
7. She borrowed money from Krogstad
8. Lawyer from whom Nora borrowed money
9. Helmer was to get a promotion to manager of the _____ right after New Years
10. Krogstad wrote one to blackmail Helmer into letting him keep his job
11. Krogstad wrote a letter to ____ Helmer
12. I've been wronged greatly, Torvald--first by ____ and then by you.
13. Nora borrowed money to finance a trip to Italy for him
14. Does your husband's love for you run so ____?
15. Mrs. Linde gave Krogstad ____ for the future
16. They don't inquire into motives

A=7	B=11	C=6	D=10
E=14	F=2	G=15	H=3
I=12	J=8	K=9	L=5
M=1	N=13	O=4	P=16

A Doll's House Magic Squares 2

Match the definition with the vocabulary word. Put your answers in the magic squares below. When your answers are correct, all columns and rows will add to the same number.

A. SUICIDE
B. ACT
C. BLACKMAIL
D. THIN
E. CHILDREN
F. FORGED
G. APPEARANCES
H. LOAN
I. MORAL
J. PROMOTION
K. LINDE
L. LAWS
M. LOVE
N. KROGSTAD
O. BANK
P. HOPE

1. At the end of Act Two Nora decided to commit it
2. Lawyer from whom Nora borrowed money
3. Helmer was expecting one at the beginning of the new year
4. Nora didn't want to see hers at the end of Act One
5. Nora realized Helmer was more concerned with this than with her
6. They don't inquire into motives
7. Mrs. Linde gave Krogstad ____ for the future
8. Krogstad wrote a letter to ____ Helmer
9. Helmer was to get a promotion to manager of the ____ right after New Years
10. Does your husband's love for you run so ____?
11. Nora got one from Krogstad
12. Old friend of Nora; hopes to get a job at the bank
13. His ____ failings I could maybe overlook if I had to
14. Nora ____ her father's signature on the note
15. Play division
16. Dr. Rank declared his ____ for Nora

A=	B=	C=	D=
E=	F=	G=	H=
I=	J=	K=	L=
M=	N=	O=	P=

A Doll's House Magic Squares 2 Answer Key

Match the definition with the vocabulary word. Put your answers in the magic squares below. When your answers are correct, all columns and rows will add to the same number.

A. SUICIDE
B. ACT
C. BLACKMAIL
D. THIN
E. CHILDREN
F. FORGED
G. APPEARANCES
H. LOAN
I. MORAL
J. PROMOTION
K. LINDE
L. LAWS
M. LOVE
N. KROGSTAD
O. BANK
P. HOPE

1. At the end of Act Two Nora decided to commit it
2. Lawyer from whom Nora borrowed money
3. Helmer was expecting one at the beginning of the new year
4. Nora didn't want to see hers at the end of Act One
5. Nora realized Helmer was more concerned with this than with her
6. They don't inquire into motives
7. Mrs. Linde gave Krogstad ____ for the future
8. Krogstad wrote a letter to ____ Helmer
9. Helmer was to get a promotion to manager of the ____ right after New Years
10. Does your husband's love for you run so ____?
11. Nora got one from Krogstad
12. Old friend of Nora; hopes to get a job at the bank
13. His ____ failings I could maybe overlook if I had to
14. Nora ____ her father's signature on the note
15. Play division
16. Dr. Rank declared his ____ for Nora

A=1	B=15	C=8	D=10
E=4	F=14	G=5	H=11
I=13	J=3	K=12	L=6
M=16	N=2	O=9	P=7

A Doll's House Magic Squares 3

Match the definition with the vocabulary word. Put your answers in the magic squares below. When your answers are correct, all columns and rows will add to the same number.

A. KROGSTAD
B. HELMER
C. FORGED
D. COPYING
E. MOTHER
F. HOPE
G. THIN
H. LARK
I. JUSTICE
J. APPEARANCES
K. SUICIDE
L. PEOPLE
M. NORA
N. LINDE
O. SCENE
P. DOLL

1. Mrs. Linde gave Krogstad ____ for the future
2. And then to suffer this way for somebody else's sins. Is there any ____ in that?
3. Act division
4. Extra work Nora took on to help pay off the loan
5. She borrowed money from Krogstad
6. Nora's husband
7. What's become of the little ____?
8. At the end of Act Two Nora decided to commit it
9. Nora ____ her father's signature on the note
10. A ____'s House
11. Nora realized Helmer was more concerned with this than with her
12. Most everyone who goes bad early in life had a ____ who's a chronic liar
13. And you're not even thinking what ____ will say
14. Does your husband's love for you run so ____?
15. Lawyer from whom Nora borrowed money
16. Old friend of Nora; hopes to get a job at the bank

A=	B=	C=	D=
E=	F=	G=	H=
I=	J=	K=	L=
M=	N=	O=	P=

A Doll's House Magic Squares 3 Answer Key

Match the definition with the vocabulary word. Put your answers in the magic squares below. When your answers are correct, all columns and rows will add to the same number.

A. KROGSTAD
B. HELMER
C. FORGED
D. COPYING
E. MOTHER
F. HOPE
G. THIN
H. LARK
I. JUSTICE
J. APPEARANCES
K. SUICIDE
L. PEOPLE
M. NORA
N. LINDE
O. SCENE
P. DOLL

1. Mrs. Linde gave Krogstad ____ for the future
2. And then to suffer this way for somebody else's sins. Is there any ____ in that?
3. Act division
4. Extra work Nora took on to help pay off the loan
5. She borrowed money from Krogstad
6. Nora's husband
7. What's become of the little ____?
8. At the end of Act Two Nora decided to commit it
9. Nora ____ her father's signature on the note
10. A ____'s House
11. Nora realized Helmer was more concerned with this than with her
12. Most everyone who goes bad early in life had a ____ who's a chronic liar
13. And you're not even thinking what ____ will say
14. Does your husband's love for you run so ____?
15. Lawyer from whom Nora borrowed money
16. Old friend of Nora; hopes to get a job at the bank

A=15	B=6	C=9	D=4
E=12	F=1	G=14	H=7
I=2	J=11	K=8	L=13
M=5	N=16	O=3	P=10

A Doll's House Magic Squares 4

Match the definition with the vocabulary word. Put your answers in the magic squares below. When your answers are correct, all columns and rows will add to the same number.

A. HELMER
B. LETTER
C. CHILDREN
D. STAGE
E. DOLL
F. MORAL
G. SCENE
H. RANK
I. LAWS
J. IBSEN
K. MOTHER
L. ITALY
M. COPYING
N. JUSTICE
O. PAPA
P. THIN

1. Nora didn't want to see hers at the end of Act One
2. Author
3. His ____ failings I could maybe overlook if I had to
4. I've been wronged greatly, Torvald--first by ____ and then by you.
5. Does your husband's love for you run so ____?
6. A ____'s House
7. They don't inquire into motives
8. Place where a play is put on
9. Extra work Nora took on to help pay off the loan
10. Doctor who has a terminal disease
11. Country where Torvald went to recover
12. Nora's husband
13. Krogstad wrote one to blackmail Helmer into letting him keep his job
14. Most everyone who goes bad early in life had a ____ who's a chronic liar
15. Act division
16. And then to suffer this way for somebody else's sins. Is there any ____ in that? ____ in that?

A=	B=	C=	D=
E=	F=	G=	H=
I=	J=	K=	L=
M=	N=	O=	P=

27
Copyrighted

A Doll's House Magic Squares 4 Answer Key

Match the definition with the vocabulary word. Put your answers in the magic squares below. When your answers are correct, all columns and rows will add to the same number.

A. HELMER
B. LETTER
C. CHILDREN
D. STAGE
E. DOLL
F. MORAL

G. SCENE
H. RANK
I. LAWS
J. IBSEN
K. MOTHER
L. ITALY

M. COPYING
N. JUSTICE
O. PAPA
P. THIN

1. Nora didn't want to see hers at the end of Act One
2. Author
3. His ____ failings I could maybe overlook if I had to
4. I've been wronged greatly, Torvald--first by ____ and then by you.
5. Does your husband's love for you run so ____?
6. A ____'s House
7. They don't inquire into motives
8. Place where a play is put on
9. Extra work Nora took on to help pay off the loan
10. Doctor who has a terminal disease
11. Country where Torvald went to recover
12. Nora's husband
13. Krogstad wrote one to blackmail Helmer into letting him keep his job
14. Most everyone who goes bad early in life had a ____ who's a chronic liar
15. Act division
16. And then to suffer this way for somebody else's sins. Is there any ____ in that? ____ in that?

A=12	B=13	C=1	D=8
E=6	F=3	G=15	H=10
I=7	J=2	K=14	L=11
M=9	N=16	O=4	P=5

A Doll's House Word Search 1

Words are placed backwards, forward, diagonally, up and down. Clues listed below can help you find the words. Circle the hidden vocabulary words in the maze.

```
T O R V A L D M Q M H P G V S L C A M H
H X K P F C K Y O B Z O P S U I H P R X
I D R R C J O C H T N B P C I N I P K V
N C S O P U H P Y L H Z N E C D L E C V
G F B M R S G H Y J B E R N I E D A N S
R B G O X T T Y W I S S R E D X R R H D
N T D T P I X V F B N H Q W E C E A P W
F P M I C C P V I P C G E B D H N N S H
Y V N O D E H H T D L G B Y P L Z C Y Z
G Z H N S C M X C Y A Z P Q D D K E K V
Y B R H V V Y F N T L J I J J K Y S Y X
C P P D F G S R S B Q J G T M P K Z P Y
T W D A D X S V G H N F C B A G L X A F
R L F T D J E M Q P M N B H N L R O P F
E P L S V B N T Q P K W B F K W Y H A B
T M W G Q X I M G X E N V N O H S E L N
T Z V O Y J P W O B T O A D B R F L O W
E K C R K T P S G R C B P O W L G M V C
L A R K B L A C K M A I L L A W S E E J
R A N K S Y H N O R A L D L E V S R D P
```

A ____'s House (4)
Act division (5)
And then to suffer this way for somebody else's sins. Is there any ____ in that? (7)
And you're not even thinking what ____ will say (6)
At the end of Act Two Nora decided to commit it (7)
Author (5)
Country where Torvald went to recover (5)
Doctor who has a terminal disease (4)
Does your husband's love for you run so ____? (4)
Dr. Rank declared his ____ for Nora (4)
Extra work Nora took on to help pay off the loan (7)
From now on ____ doesn't matter; all that matters is...the appearance (9)
Helmer was expecting one at the beginning of the new year (9)
Helmer was to get a promotion to manager of the _____ right after New Years (4)
His ____ failings I could maybe overlook if I had to (5)
I've been wronged greatly, Torvald--first by ____ and then by you. (4)
Krogstad wrote a letter to ____ Helmer (9)
Krogstad wrote one to blackmail Helmer into letting him keep his job (6)
Lawyer from whom Nora borrowed money (8)
Most everyone who goes bad early in life had a ____ who's a chronic liar (6)
Mrs. Linde gave Krogstad ____ for the future (4)
Nora ____ her father's signature on the note (6)
Nora borrowed money to finance a trip to Italy for him (7)
Nora didn't want to see hers at the end of Act One (8)
Nora got one from Krogstad (4)
Nora realized Helmer was more concerned with this than with her (11)
Nora's husband (6)
Old friend of Nora; hopes to get a job at the bank (5)
Place where a play is put on (5)
Play division (3)
She borrowed money from Krogstad (4)
They don't inquire into motives (4)
What's become of the little ____? (4)

A Doll's House Word Search 1 Answer Key

Words are placed backwards, forward, diagonally, up and down. Clues listed below can help you find the words. Circle the hidden vocabulary words in the maze.

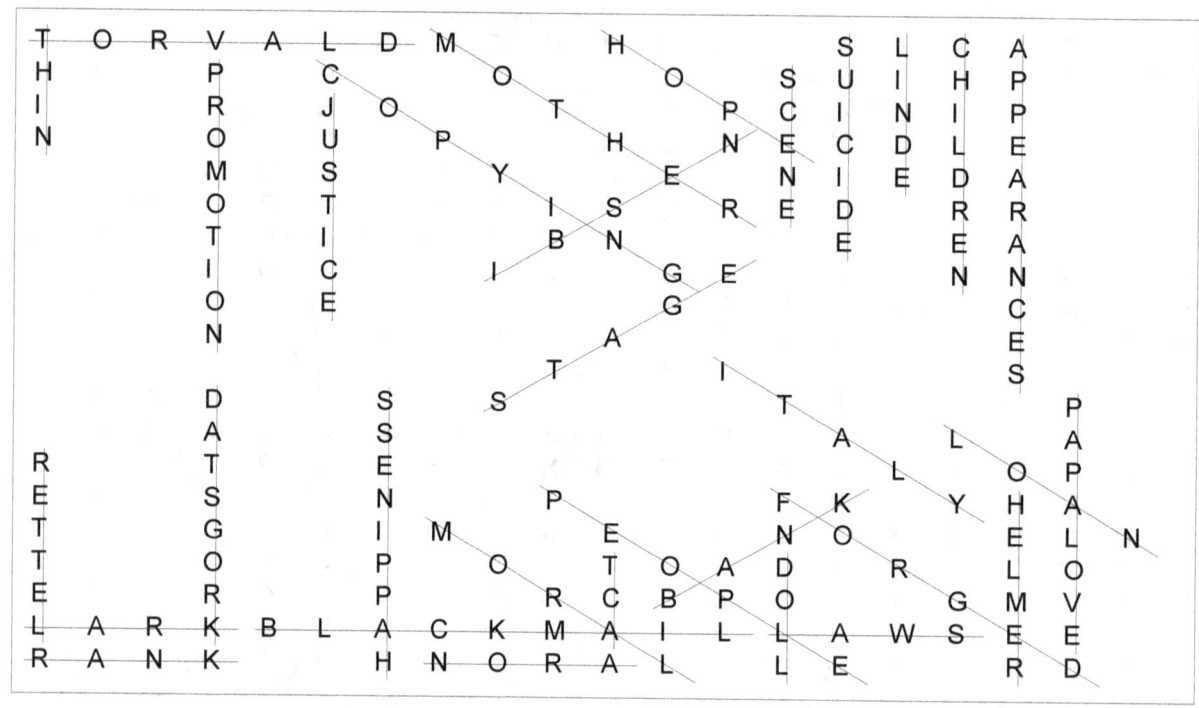

A ____'s House (4)
Act division (5)
And then to suffer this way for somebody else's sins. Is there any ____ in that? (7)
And you're not even thinking what ____ will say (6)
At the end of Act Two Nora decided to commit it (7)
Author (5)
Country where Torvald went to recover (5)
Doctor who has a terminal disease (4)
Does your husband's love for you run so ____? (4)
Dr. Rank declared his ____ for Nora (4)
Extra work Nora took on to help pay off the loan (7)
From now on ____ doesn't matter; all that matters is...the appearance (9)
Helmer was expecting one at the beginning of the new year (9)
Helmer was to get a promotion to manager of the _____ right after New Years (4)
His ____ failings I could maybe overlook if I had to (5)
I've been wronged greatly, Torvald--first by ____ and then by you. (4)
Krogstad wrote a letter to ____ Helmer (9)
Krogstad wrote one to blackmail Helmer into letting him keep his job (6)
Lawyer from whom Nora borrowed money (8)
Most everyone who goes bad early in life had a ____ who's a chronic liar (6)
Mrs. Linde gave Krogstad ____ for the future (4)
Nora ____ her father's signature on the note (6)
Nora borrowed money to finance a trip to Italy for him (7)
Nora didn't want to see hers at the end of Act One (8)
Nora got one from Krogstad (4)
Nora realized Helmer was more concerned with this than with her (11)
Nora's husband (6)
Old friend of Nora; hopes to get a job at the bank (5)
Place where a play is put on (5)
Play division (3)
She borrowed money from Krogstad (4)
They don't inquire into motives (4)
What's become of the little ____? (4)

30
Copyrighted

A Doll's House Word Search 2

Words are placed backwards, forward, diagonally, up and down. Clues listed below can help you find the words. Circle the hidden vocabulary words in the maze.

```
C R L G C M F D L G B T X P A I B S E N
O Q E X Y H X O L Z K O L R P C N G Y Q
P J T M N H I L H W N R V O P C B H H L
Y C T P L D C L F X F V D M E Z G X D X
I C E T S H K R D S M A S O A X X P Z Q
N S R D C K G T W R T L T R D G L S C
G T P Z W H R T F G E D N I A K P R F M
Y M R V Y J D G S M S N B O N H G R Q S
N M L J C U N N S H R D L N C X R L X L
H Z F C H S G R H J X S A C E Y F R W B
P C K F R T L B A P T S C B S F V W B R
W R C S S I S L P Z A D K H K O M X P C
P C N Z N C R U P D Y P M N M R B R S P
E L I N D E T H I N H D A T S G O R K X
O H G V M F N M N C W R I L R E W Y E W
P C O L S T Q B E M I W L O R D I K G K
L V E P C D S K S B O D Z A P K T B A C
E H N X E V O L S A D R E N O R A C T K
Z R N S N C Z J P N K T A X V A L W S R
M O T H E R V Y M K S W A L J L Y R S K
```

A ____'s House (4)
Act division (5)
And then to suffer this way for somebody else's sins. Is there any ____ in that? (7)
And you're not even thinking what ____ will say (6)
At the end of Act Two Nora decided to commit it (7)
Author (5)
Country where Torvald went to recover (5)
Doctor who has a terminal disease (4)
Does your husband's love for you run so ____? (4)
Dr. Rank declared his ____ for Nora (4)
Extra work Nora took on to help pay off the loan (7)
From now on ____ doesn't matter; all that matters is...the appearance (9)
Helmer was expecting one at the beginning of the new year (9)
Helmer was to get a promotion to manager of the _____ right after New Years (4)
His ____ failings I could maybe overlook if I had to (5)
I've been wronged greatly, Torvald--first by ____ and then by you. (4)
Krogstad wrote a letter to ____ Helmer (9)
Krogstad wrote one to blackmail Helmer into letting him keep his job (6)
Lawyer from whom Nora borrowed money (8)
Most everyone who goes bad early in life had a ____ who's a chronic liar (6)
Mrs. Linde gave Krogstad ____ for the future (4)
Nora ____ her father's signature on the note (6)
Nora borrowed money to finance a trip to Italy for him (7)
Nora didn't want to see hers at the end of Act One (8)
Nora got one from Krogstad (4)
Nora realized Helmer was more concerned with this than with her (11)
Nora's husband (6)
Old friend of Nora; hopes to get a job at the bank (5)
Place where a play is put on (5)
Play division (3)
She borrowed money from Krogstad (4)
They don't inquire into motives (4)
What's become of the little ____? (4)

A Doll's House Word Search 2 Answer Key

Words are placed backwards, forward, diagonally, up and down. Clues listed below can help you find the words. Circle the hidden vocabulary words in the maze.

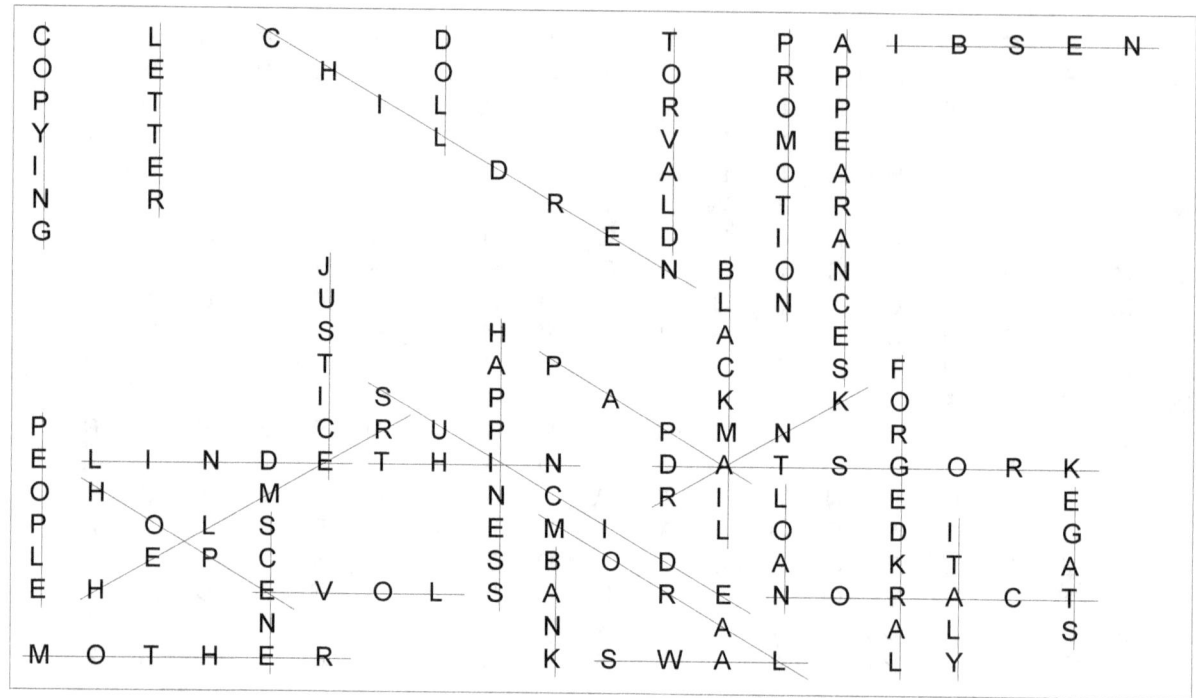

A ____'s House (4)
Act division (5)
And then to suffer this way for somebody else's sins. Is there any ____ in that? (7)
And you're not even thinking what ____ will say (6)
At the end of Act Two Nora decided to commit it (7)
Author (5)
Country where Torvald went to recover (5)
Doctor who has a terminal disease (4)
Does your husband's love for you run so ____? (4)
Dr. Rank declared his ____ for Nora (4)
Extra work Nora took on to help pay off the loan (7)
From now on ____ doesn't matter; all that matters is...the appearance (9)
Helmer was expecting one at the beginning of the new year (9)
Helmer was to get a promotion to manager of the _____ right after New Years (4)
His ____ failings I could maybe overlook if I had to (5)
I've been wronged greatly, Torvald--first by ____ and then by you. (4)
Krogstad wrote a letter to ____ Helmer (9)
Krogstad wrote one to blackmail Helmer into letting him keep his job (6)
Lawyer from whom Nora borrowed money (8)
Most everyone who goes bad early in life had a ____ who's a chronic liar (6)
Mrs. Linde gave Krogstad ____ for the future (4)
Nora ____ her father's signature on the note (6)
Nora borrowed money to finance a trip to Italy for him (7)
Nora didn't want to see hers at the end of Act One (8)
Nora got one from Krogstad (4)
Nora realized Helmer was more concerned with this than with her (11)
Nora's husband (6)
Old friend of Nora; hopes to get a job at the bank (5)
Place where a play is put on (5)
Play division (3)
She borrowed money from Krogstad (4)
They don't inquire into motives (4)
What's become of the little ____? (4)

A Doll's House Word Search 3

Words are placed backwards, forward, diagonally, up and down. Words listed below are included in the maze. Circle the hidden vocabulary words in the maze.

```
F O R G E D Y B C G Y I K R O G S T A D
J H N R P Y J L C H Q T R H R F R P C J
G A Z V K K W A Z O K A S H F X P Q X T
C P G Z N B Z C K F P L R R D E H G B V
K P T A W L F K J S N Y E F A J F N R H
P I B F S C W M L Z R H I R Q P Q F P T
W N F K V W J A H T T G A N L F P M D D
L E J L Z H U I N O W N F R G N M X R W
L S S V W N S L M B C G H C G I H W B B
W S B T V M T T N E Z X Z N V C B X J L
M G H Y A Z I M S J P T T F F C G S W O
F G Z Y W G C R T P Z O Y Y T L Q L E A
L I N D E H E L M E R V C H I L D R E N
S F V M Q T J Y Z V N O I H L T R J F J
U W Z B T W W R A C O N M P O A Z L S Y
I Z V E W W Q L Y L R N L O E P R T W C
C C L A C T D O L L A R H O T O E K P V
I D G P R D Q L N W T W A W V I P W N P
D P L A N M V T K N K T S N Z E O L Z Y
E R R P M O R A L S C E N E K B X N E N
```

ACT   HELMER   LINDE   RANK

APPEARANCES   HOPE   LOAN   SCENE

BANK   IBSEN   LOVE   STAGE

BLACKMAIL   ITALY   MORAL   SUICIDE

CHILDREN   JUSTICE   MOTHER   THIN

COPYING   KROGSTAD   NORA   TORVALD

DOLL   LARK   PAPA

FORGED   LAWS   PEOPLE

HAPPINESS   LETTER   PROMOTION

A Doll's House Word Search 3 Answer Key

Words are placed backwards, forward, diagonally, up and down. Words listed below are included in the maze. Circle the hidden vocabulary words in the maze.

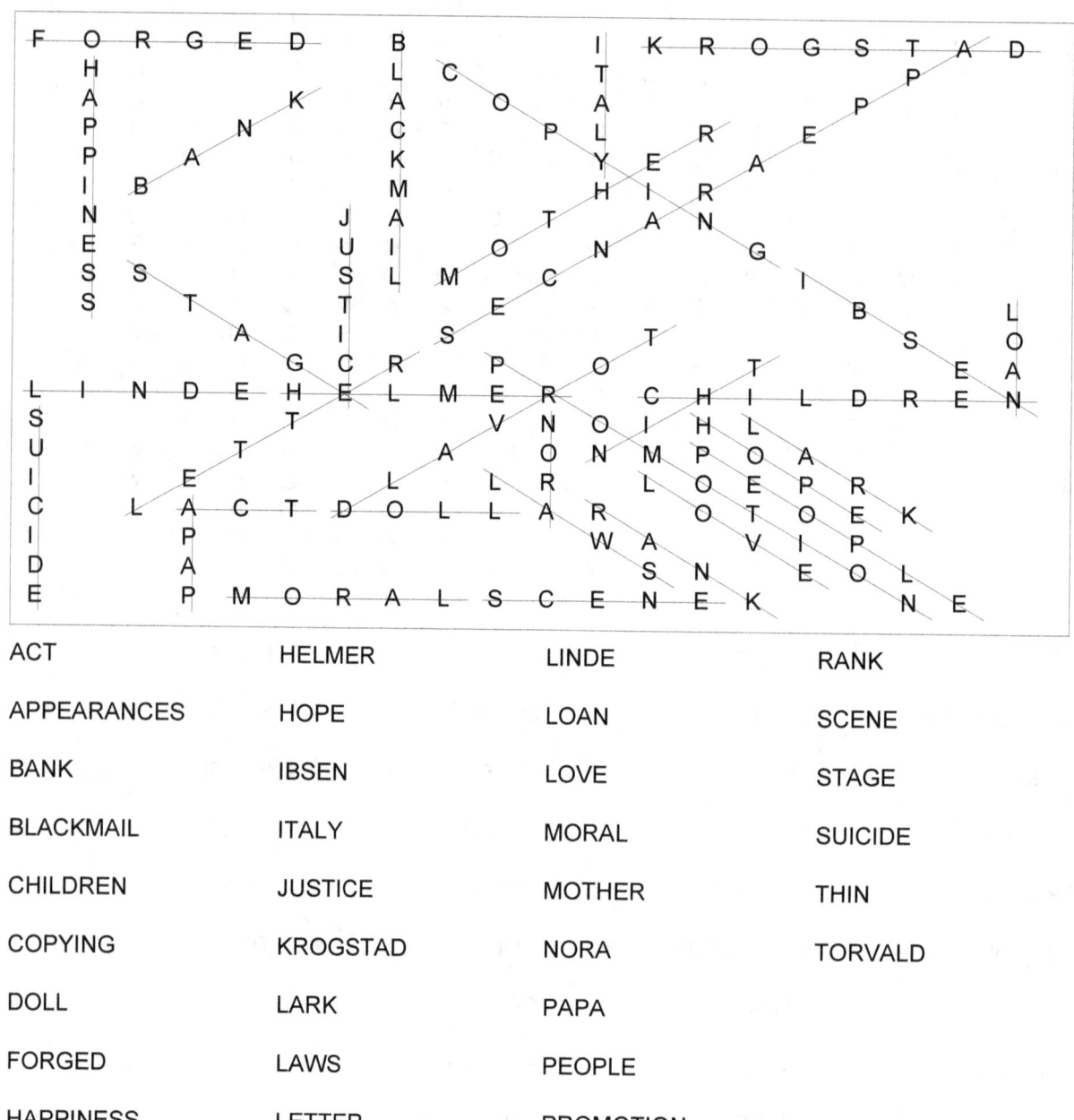

ACT	HELMER	LINDE	RANK
APPEARANCES	HOPE	LOAN	SCENE
BANK	IBSEN	LOVE	STAGE
BLACKMAIL	ITALY	MORAL	SUICIDE
CHILDREN	JUSTICE	MOTHER	THIN
COPYING	KROGSTAD	NORA	TORVALD
DOLL	LARK	PAPA	
FORGED	LAWS	PEOPLE	
HAPPINESS	LETTER	PROMOTION	

A Doll's House Word Search 4

Words are placed backwards, forward, diagonally, up and down. Words listed below are included in the maze. Circle the hidden vocabulary words in the maze.

```
P H J F G P Q L A P P E A R A N C E S Y
B T F V T C X S F D F S V F J D B R S D
C R L F M H Q C S J Z O N Z C T K J S H
K X G F G Q D G U D R S R R K K H R C R
D D N D S L Q M I S C Q N G T Y K I E H
T L R X A T K W C W F H O P E M L D N P
K A S V G W A T I L C K Y D H D K O E D
L R R F F J Z G D Z Q G N H L N R G B W
X O H A P P I N E S S I K T C A J J D P
T M V Q M R E W Z B L R L Y X O R A C C
I M F E D O M O J Z W T F E F L T K O P
J T C N Q M B J P D O L L M T S F N P S
U K A H W O O L P L F B G L G T N A Y W
S R W L S T Z T A S E T D O K I E R I Z
T K B K Y I S H H C N P R G P Z B R N F
I R J J Q O F E V E K K Z Y J A M S G S
C H F S X N D L W F R M K Z C M P Q E T
E M W K G T L M R L Y N A X D M Z A R N
V A P D D H J E Z T A C H I L D R E N X
L B P V S B M R Q B N J J W L H H Y Q X
```

ACT	HELMER	LINDE	RANK
APPEARANCES	HOPE	LOAN	SCENE
BANK	IBSEN	LOVE	STAGE
BLACKMAIL	ITALY	MORAL	SUICIDE
CHILDREN	JUSTICE	MOTHER	THIN
COPYING	KROGSTAD	NORA	TORVALD
DOLL	LARK	PAPA	
FORGED	LAWS	PEOPLE	
HAPPINESS	LETTER	PROMOTION	

A Doll's House Word Search 4 Answer Key

Words are placed backwards, forward, diagonally, up and down. Words listed below are included in the maze. Circle the hidden vocabulary words in the maze.

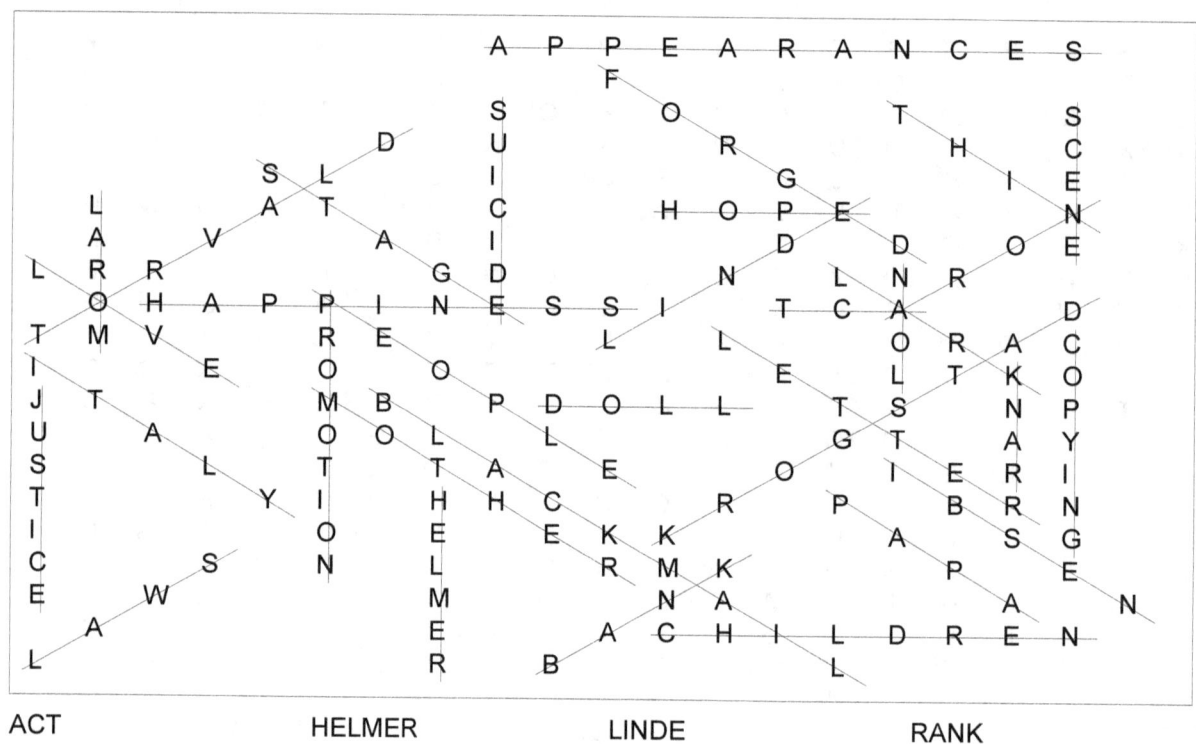

ACT	HELMER	LINDE	RANK
APPEARANCES	HOPE	LOAN	SCENE
BANK	IBSEN	LOVE	STAGE
BLACKMAIL	ITALY	MORAL	SUICIDE
CHILDREN	JUSTICE	MOTHER	THIN
COPYING	KROGSTAD	NORA	TORVALD
DOLL	LARK	PAPA	
FORGED	LAWS	PEOPLE	
HAPPINESS	LETTER	PROMOTION	

A Doll's House Crossword 1

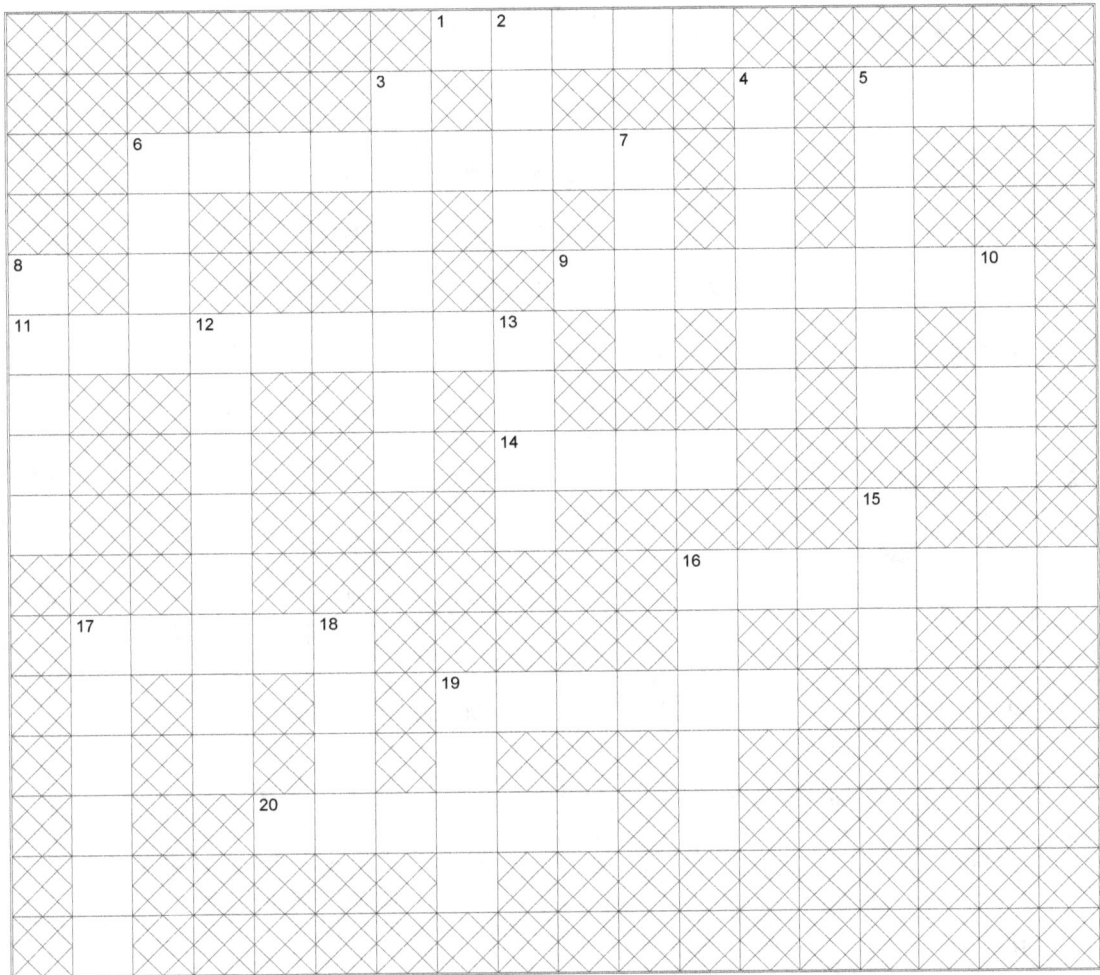

Across
1. Place where a play is put on
5. Nora got one from Krogstad
6. Helmer was expecting one at the beginning of the new year
9. Lawyer from whom Nora borrowed money
11. Krogstad wrote a letter to ____ Helmer
14. Doctor who has a terminal disease
16. At the end of Act Two Nora decided to commit it
17. His ____ failings I could maybe overlook if I had to
19. Nora's husband
20. And you're not even thinking what ____ will say

Down
2. Does your husband's love for you run so ____?
3. Nora borrowed money to finance a trip to Italy for him
4. Nora ____ her father's signature on the note
5. Krogstad wrote one to blackmail Helmer into letting him keep his job
6. I've been wronged greatly, Torvald--first by ____ and then by you.
7. She borrowed money from Krogstad
8. Author
10. A ____'s House
12. Nora didn't want to see hers at the end of Act One
13. What's become of the little ____?
15. Play division
16. Act division
17. Most everyone who goes bad early in life had a ____ who's a chronic liar
18. Dr. Rank declared his ____ for Nora
19. Mrs. Linde gave Krogstad ____ for the future

A Doll's House Crossword 1 Answer Key

						¹S	²T	A	G	E				
					³T		H			⁴F	⁵L	O	A	N
		⁶P	R	O	M	O	T	I	⁷O	N		O	E	
			A		R		N		O		R		T	
⁸I		P			V		⁹K	R	O	G	S	T	A	¹⁰D
¹¹B	¹²L	A	C	K	M	A	I	¹³L		A		E	E	O
S		C			H			L		A		D	R	L
E		H			I			D		¹⁴R	A	N	K	L
N		I			L								¹⁵A	L
		L			D					¹⁶S	U	I	C	I	D	E
	¹⁷M	O	R	A	¹⁸L					C		¹⁹T	
	O		E		O		¹⁹H	E	L	M	E	R		
	T		N		V		O			N				
	H		²⁰P	E	O	P	L	E		E				
	E				E									
	R													

Across
1. Place where a play is put on
5. Nora got one from Krogstad
6. Helmer was expecting one at the beginning of the new year
9. Lawyer from whom Nora borrowed money
11. Krogstad wrote a letter to ____ Helmer
14. Doctor who has a terminal disease
16. At the end of Act Two Nora decided to commit it
17. His ____ failings I could maybe overlook if I had to
19. Nora's husband
20. And you're not even thinking what ____ will say

Down
2. Does your husband's love for you run so ____?
3. Nora borrowed money to finance a trip to Italy for him
4. Nora ____ her father's signature on the note
5. Krogstad wrote one to blackmail Helmer into letting him keep his job
6. I've been wronged greatly, Torvald--first by ____ and then by you.
7. She borrowed money from Krogstad
8. Author
10. A ____'s House
12. Nora didn't want to see hers at the end of Act One
13. What's become of the little ____?
15. Play division
16. Act division
17. Most everyone who goes bad early in life had a ____ who's a chronic liar
18. Dr. Rank declared his ____ for Nora
19. Mrs. Linde gave Krogstad ____ for the future

A Doll's House Crossword 2

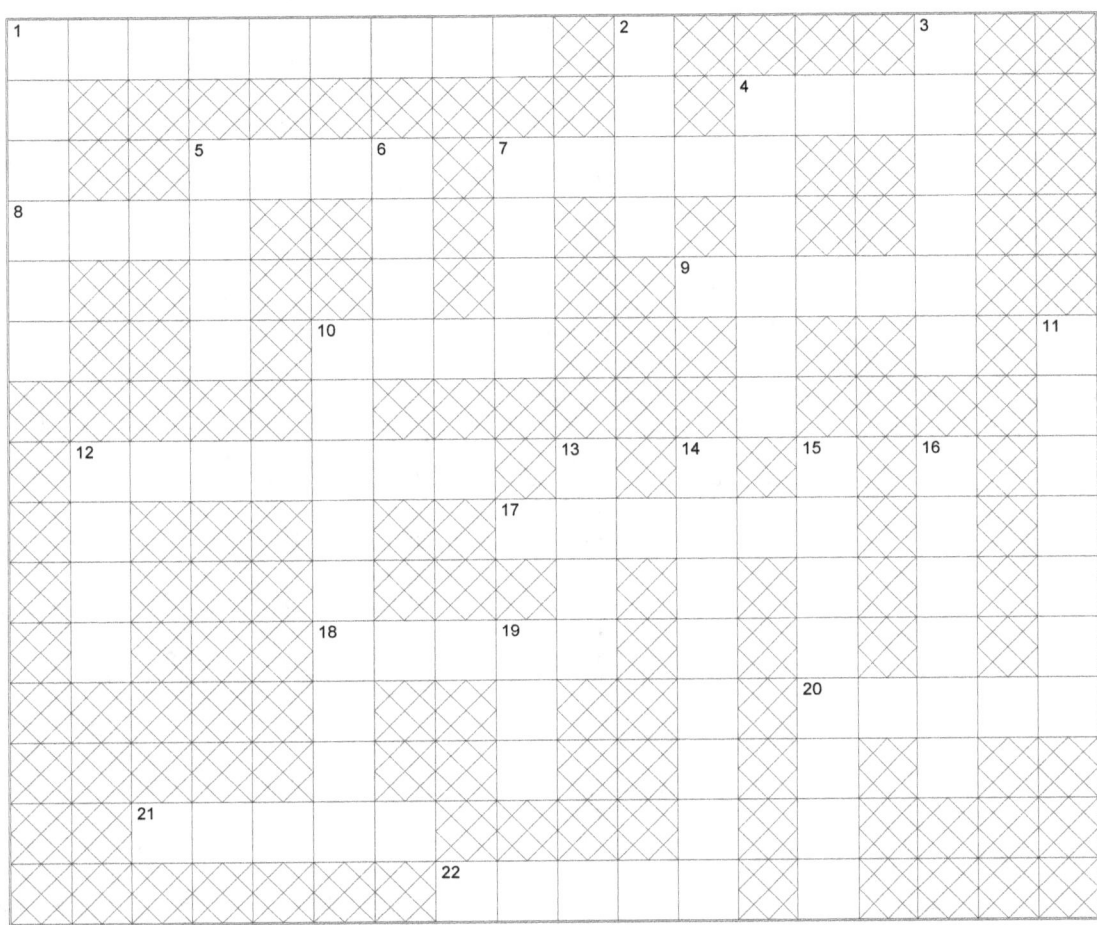

Across
1. Helmer was expecting one at the beginning of the new year
4. Dr. Rank declared his ____ for Nora
5. Nora got one from Krogstad
7. Old friend of Nora; hopes to get a job at the bank
8. I've been wronged greatly, Torvald--first by ____ and then by you.
9. Place where a play is put on
10. Helmer was to get a promotion to manager of the ____ right after New Years
12. Nora borrowed money to finance a trip to Italy for him
17. Most everyone who goes bad early in life had a ____ who's a chronic liar
18. His ____ failings I could maybe overlook if I had to
20. Act division
21. Country where Torvald went to recover
22. Author

Down
1. And you're not even thinking what ____ will say
2. Doctor who has a terminal disease
3. Nora's husband
4. Krogstad wrote one to blackmail Helmer into letting him keep his job
5. They don't inquire into motives
6. She borrowed money from Krogstad
7. What's become of the little ____?
10. Krogstad wrote a letter to ____ Helmer
11. At the end of Act Two Nora decided to commit it
12. Does your husband's love for you run so ____?
13. A ____'s House
14. Nora didn't want to see hers at the end of Act One
15. Lawyer from whom Nora borrowed money
16. Nora ____ her father's signature on the note
19. Play division

A Doll's House Crossword 2 Answer Key

	1								2				3	
	P	R	O	M	O	T	I	O	N				H	
	E							4	R					
									A		L	O	V	E
	O			5		6		7					E	
				L	O	A	N	L	I	N	D	E	L	
	8													
	P	A	P	A		O		A		K	T		M	
	L			W		R		R		9	S	T	A	G	E
	E			S		10					E		R		11 S
						B	A	N	K					
						L					R				U
	12							13		14		15		16	
	T	O	R	V	A	L	D		D		C		K		F	I
	H					C		17 M	O	T	H	E	R		O	C
	I					K			L		I		O		R	I
						18		19								
	N					M	O	R	A	L		L		G		G	D
						A			C			D		20 S	C	E	N	E
						I			T			R		T		D	
				21 I	T	A	L	Y				E		A			
								22 I	B	S	E	N		D			

Across

1. Helmer was expecting one at the beginning of the new year
4. Dr. Rank declared his ____ for Nora
5. Nora got one from Krogstad
7. Old friend of Nora; hopes to get a job at the bank
8. I've been wronged greatly, Torvald--first by ____ and then by you.
9. Place where a play is put on
10. Helmer was to get a promotion to manager of the _____ right after New Years
12. Nora borrowed money to finance a trip to Italy for him
17. Most everyone who goes bad early in life had a ____ who's a chronic liar
18. His ____ failings I could maybe overlook if I had to
20. Act division
21. Country where Torvald went to recover
22. Author

Down

1. And you're not even thinking what ____ will say
2. Doctor who has a terminal disease
3. Nora's husband
4. Krogstad wrote one to blackmail Helmer into letting him keep his job
5. They don't inquire into motives
6. She borrowed money from Krogstad
7. What's become of the little ____?
10. Krogstad wrote a letter to ____ Helmer
11. At the end of Act Two Nora decided to commit it
12. Does your husband's love for you run so ____?
13. A ____'s House
14. Nora didn't want to see hers at the end of Act One
15. Lawyer from whom Nora borrowed money
16. Nora ____ her father's signature on the note
19. Play division

A Doll's House Crossword 3

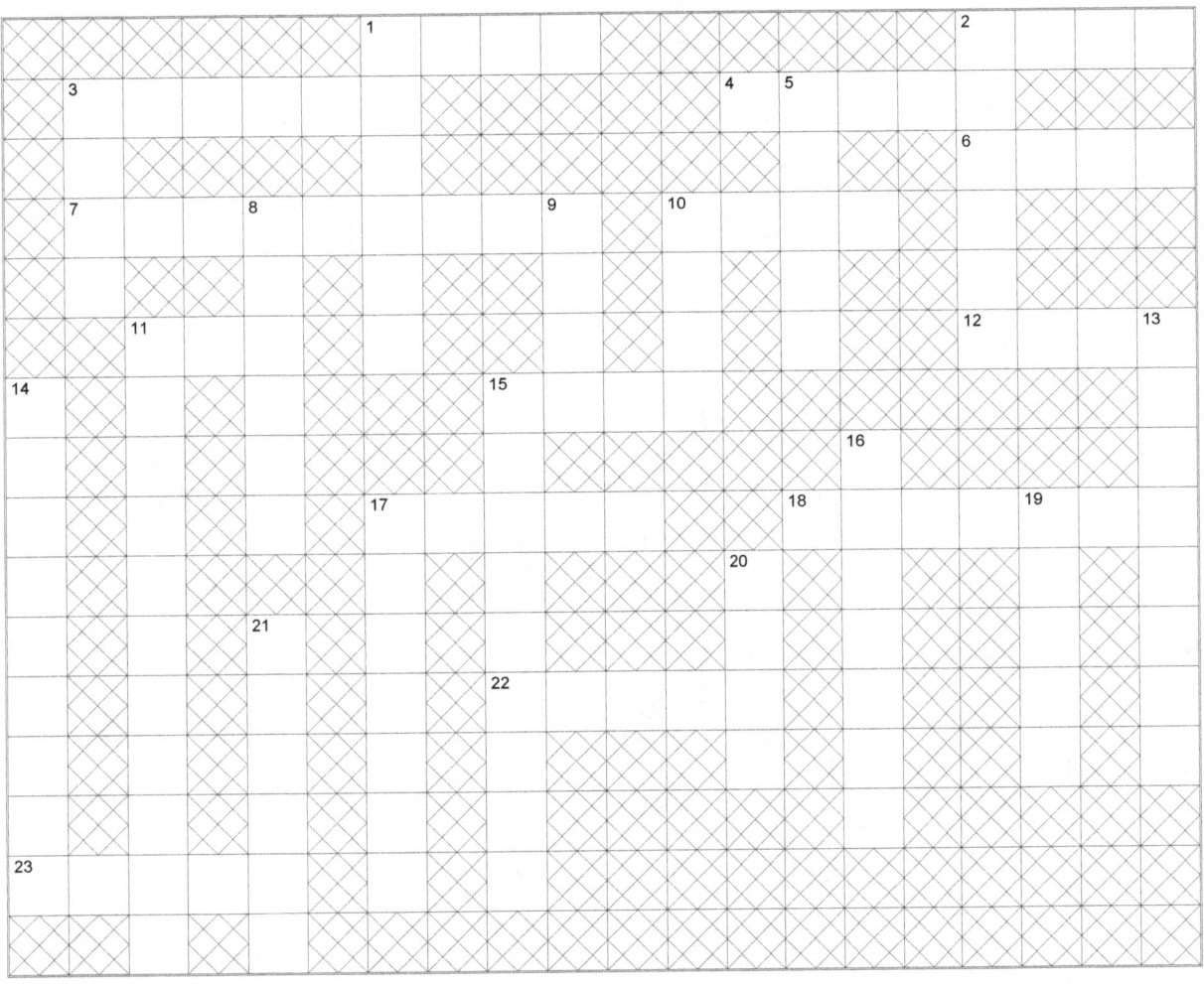

Across
1. They don't inquire into motives
2. Mrs. Linde gave Krogstad ____ for the future
3. And you're not even thinking what ____ will say
4. Old friend of Nora; hopes to get a job at the bank
6. Dr. Rank declared his ____ for Nora
7. Helmer was expecting one at the beginning of the new year
10. Nora got one from Krogstad
11. Play division
12. Doctor who has a terminal disease
15. Helmer was to get a promotion to manager of the _____ right after New Years
17. Place where a play is put on
18. Extra work Nora took on to help pay off the loan
22. His ____ failings I could maybe overlook if I had to
23. Act division

Down
1. Krogstad wrote one to blackmail Helmer into letting him keep his job
2. Nora's husband
3. I've been wronged greatly, Torvald--first by ____ and then by you.
5. Country where Torvald went to recover
8. Most everyone who goes bad early in life had a ____ who's a chronic liar
9. She borrowed money from Krogstad
10. What's become of the little ____?
11. Nora realized Helmer was more concerned with this than with her
13. Lawyer from whom Nora borrowed money
14. From now on ____ doesn't matter; all that matters is...the appearance
15. Krogstad wrote a letter to ____ Helmer
16. Nora borrowed money to finance a trip to Italy for him
17. At the end of Act Two Nora decided to commit it
19. Author
20. A ____'s House
21. Nora ____ her father's signature on the note

A Doll's House Crossword 3 Answer Key

						¹L	A	W	S					²H	O	P	E
	³P	E	O	P	L	E				⁴L	⁵I	N	D	E			
	A					T					T			⁶L	O	V	E
⁷P	R	O	⁸M	O	T	I	O	N		⁹L	¹⁰O	A	N		M		
A			O		E			O		A			L		E		
	¹¹A	C	T		R			R		R		¹²R	A	N	¹³K		
¹⁴H	P		H			¹⁵B	A	N	K				Y				R
A	P		E			L					¹⁶T						O
P	E		R		¹⁷S	T	A	G	E		¹⁸C	O	P	Y	¹⁹I	N	G
P	A				U		C			²⁰D		R			B		S
I	R		²¹F		I		K			O		V			S		T
N	A		O		C		²²M	O	R	A	L				E		A
E	N		R		I		A			L		L			N		D
S	C		G		D		I			L		D					
²³S	C	E	N	E			L										
			S		D												

Across
1. They don't inquire into motives
2. Mrs. Linde gave Krogstad ____ for the future
3. And you're not even thinking what ____ will say
4. Old friend of Nora; hopes to get a job at the bank
6. Dr. Rank declared his ____ for Nora
7. Helmer was expecting one at the beginning of the new year
10. Nora got one from Krogstad
11. Play division
12. Doctor who has a terminal disease
15. Helmer was to get a promotion to manager of the _____ right after New Years
17. Place where a play is put on
18. Extra work Nora took on to help pay off the loan
22. His ____ failings I could maybe overlook if I had to
23. Act division

Down
1. Krogstad wrote one to blackmail Helmer into letting him keep his job
2. Nora's husband
3. I've been wronged greatly, Torvald--first by ____ and then by you.
5. Country where Torvald went to recover
8. Most everyone who goes bad early in life had a ____ who's a chronic liar
9. She borrowed money from Krogstad
10. What's become of the little ____?
11. Nora realized Helmer was more concerned with this than with her
13. Lawyer from whom Nora borrowed money
14. From now on ____ doesn't matter; all that matters is...the appearance
15. Krogstad wrote a letter to ____ Helmer
16. Nora borrowed money to finance a trip to Italy for him
17. At the end of Act Two Nora decided to commit it
19. Author
20. A ____'s House
21. Nora ____ her father's signature on the note

A Doll's House Crossword 4

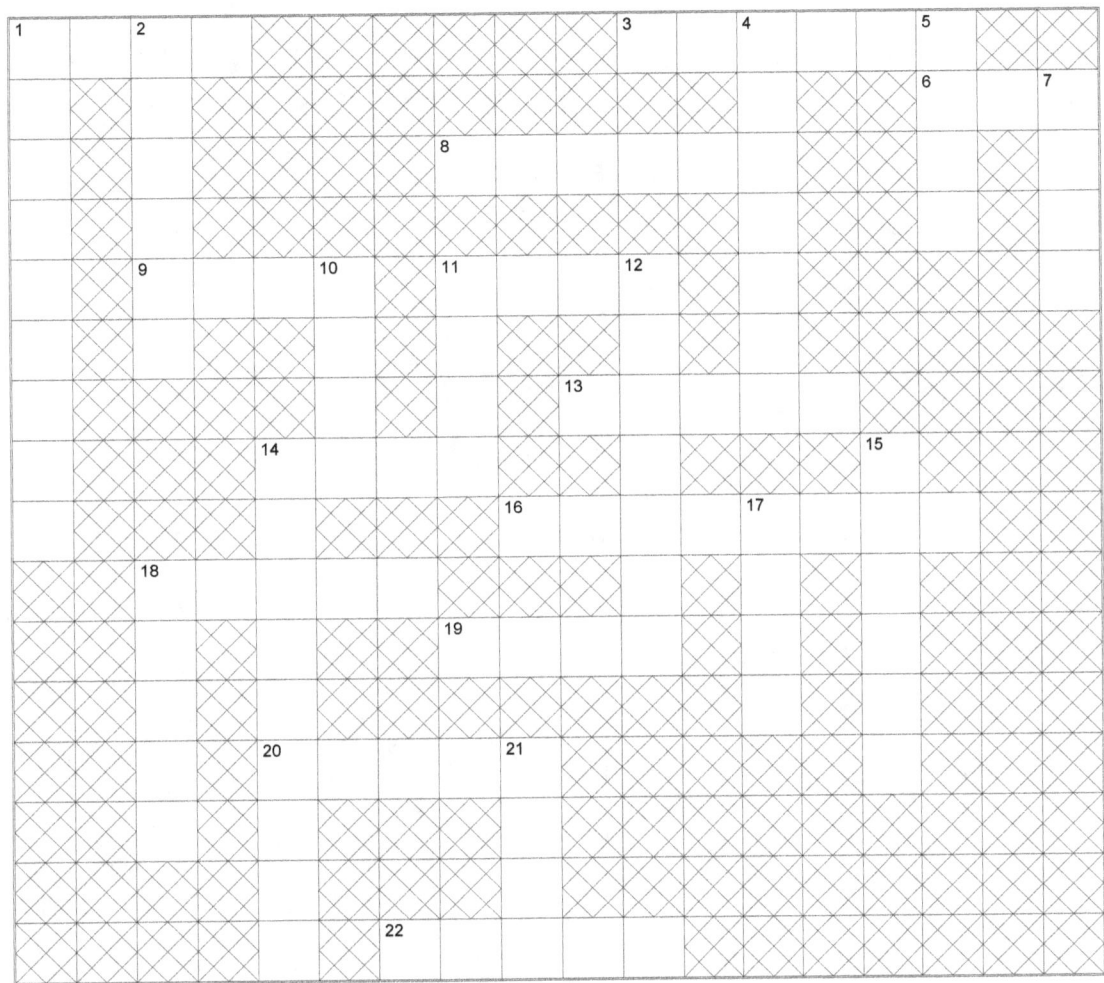

Across
1. I've been wronged greatly, Torvald--first by ____ and then by you.
3. Most everyone who goes bad early in life had a ____ who's a chronic liar
6. Play division
8. Krogstad wrote one to blackmail Helmer into letting him keep his job
9. Nora got one from Krogstad
11. They don't inquire into motives
13. Old friend of Nora; hopes to get a job at the bank
14. Helmer was to get a promotion to manager of the ____ right after New Years
16. Nora didn't want to see hers at the end of Act One
18. Country where Torvald went to recover
19. Mrs. Linde gave Krogstad ____ for the future
20. His ____ failings I could maybe overlook if I had to
22. Act division

Down
1. Helmer was expecting one at the beginning of the new year
2. And you're not even thinking what ____ will say
4. Nora borrowed money to finance a trip to Italy for him
5. Doctor who has a terminal disease
7. Does your husband's love for you run so ____?
10. She borrowed money from Krogstad
11. What's become of the little ____?
12. At the end of Act Two Nora decided to commit it
14. Krogstad wrote a letter to ____ Helmer
15. Nora's husband
17. A ____'s House
18. Author
21. Dr. Rank declared his ____ for Nora

A Doll's House Crossword 4 Answer Key

	1 P	2 A	P	A			3 M	4 O	T	H	5 E	R	
	R	E						O				6 A	7 T
	O	O			8 L	E	T	T	E	R		N	H
	M	P						V				K	I
	9 O	L	10 O	A	11 N	L	12 A	W	S		A		N
	T	E			O		A		U		L		
	I				R		R		13 L	I	N	D	E
	O			14 B	A	N	K		C			15 H	
	N			L				16 C	H	I	17 L	D	R	E	N
			18 I	T	A	L	Y			D		O	L
			B		C		19 H	O	P	E		L	M
			S		K					L		L	E
			20 E		M	O	R	21 A	L				R
			N		A			L					
					I			O					
				22 L		S	C	E	N	E			

Across
1. I've been wronged greatly, Torvald--first by ____ and then by you.
3. Most everyone who goes bad early in life had a ____ who's a chronic liar
6. Play division
8. Krogstad wrote one to blackmail Helmer into letting him keep his job
9. Nora got one from Krogstad
11. They don't inquire into motives
13. Old friend of Nora; hopes to get a job at the bank
14. Helmer was to get a promotion to manager of the ____ right after New Years
16. Nora didn't want to see hers at the end of Act One
18. Country where Torvald went to recover
19. Mrs. Linde gave Krogstad ____ for the future
20. His ____ failings I could maybe overlook if I had to
22. Act division

Down
1. Helmer was expecting one at the beginning of the new year
2. And you're not even thinking what ____ will say
4. Nora borrowed money to finance a trip to Italy for him
5. Doctor who has a terminal disease
7. Does your husband's love for you run so ____?
10. She borrowed money from Krogstad
11. What's become of the little ____?
12. At the end of Act Two Nora decided to commit it
14. Krogstad wrote a letter to ____ Helmer
15. Nora's husband
17. A ____'s House
18. Author
21. Dr. Rank declared his ____ for Nora

A Doll's House

LARK	CHILDREN	SCENE	HAPPINESS	THIN
BANK	PEOPLE	STAGE	MOTHER	COPYING
HELMER	LOAN	FREE SPACE	ACT	LETTER
HOPE	LAWS	ITALY	IBSEN	FORGED
SUICIDE	PROMOTION	LINDE	KROGSTAD	NORA

A Doll's House

DOLL	TORVALD	BLACKMAIL	RANK	MORAL
PAPA	LOVE	APPEARANCES	NORA	KROGSTAD
LINDE	PROMOTION	FREE SPACE	FORGED	IBSEN
ITALY	LAWS	HOPE	LETTER	ACT
JUSTICE	LOAN	HELMER	COPYING	MOTHER

A Doll's House

SUICIDE	HOPE	LARK	COPYING	BLACKMAIL
APPEARANCES	HELMER	HAPPINESS	STAGE	MORAL
SCENE	PEOPLE	FREE SPACE	ITALY	PAPA
TORVALD	JUSTICE	LETTER	LOAN	MOTHER
PROMOTION	THIN	LAWS	BANK	DOLL

A Doll's House

FORGED	IBSEN	RANK	ACT	KROGSTAD
LINDE	CHILDREN	NORA	DOLL	BANK
LAWS	THIN	FREE SPACE	MOTHER	LOAN
LETTER	JUSTICE	TORVALD	PAPA	ITALY
LOVE	PEOPLE	SCENE	MORAL	STAGE

A Doll's House

APPEARANCES	KROGSTAD	DOLL	JUSTICE	ACT
THIN	IBSEN	BANK	PROMOTION	LINDE
HOPE	MORAL	FREE SPACE	LETTER	CHILDREN
MOTHER	TORVALD	COPYING	FORGED	PAPA
RANK	LOAN	HAPPINESS	PEOPLE	NORA

A Doll's House

STAGE	LARK	SUICIDE	BLACKMAIL	LAWS
HELMER	LOVE	SCENE	NORA	PEOPLE
HAPPINESS	LOAN	FREE SPACE	PAPA	FORGED
COPYING	TORVALD	MOTHER	CHILDREN	LETTER
ITALY	MORAL	HOPE	LINDE	PROMOTION

A Doll's House

PROMOTION	PEOPLE	RANK	NORA	BANK
BLACKMAIL	COPYING	IBSEN	LAWS	ITALY
HELMER	JUSTICE	FREE SPACE	LOAN	KROGSTAD
LINDE	LARK	SCENE	LETTER	DOLL
LOVE	SUICIDE	MORAL	STAGE	ACT

A Doll's House

FORGED	APPEARANCES	HAPPINESS	PAPA	CHILDREN
MOTHER	HOPE	THIN	ACT	STAGE
MORAL	SUICIDE	FREE SPACE	DOLL	LETTER
SCENE	LARK	LINDE	KROGSTAD	LOAN
TORVALD	JUSTICE	HELMER	ITALY	LAWS

A Doll's House

PEOPLE	HAPPINESS	ACT	SCENE	BANK
LAWS	HELMER	IBSEN	FORGED	LOVE
STAGE	LARK	FREE SPACE	THIN	BLACKMAIL
MOTHER	CHILDREN	LINDE	LOAN	ITALY
APPEARANCES	HOPE	MORAL	JUSTICE	PROMOTION

A Doll's House

NORA	TORVALD	RANK	PAPA	DOLL
LETTER	SUICIDE	KROGSTAD	PROMOTION	JUSTICE
MORAL	HOPE	FREE SPACE	ITALY	LOAN
LINDE	CHILDREN	MOTHER	BLACKMAIL	THIN
COPYING	LARK	STAGE	LOVE	FORGED

A Doll's House

LARK	PROMOTION	ITALY	THIN	HAPPINESS
CHILDREN	DOLL	PEOPLE	SUICIDE	PAPA
COPYING	JUSTICE	FREE SPACE	MOTHER	BLACKMAIL
BANK	LINDE	LOAN	NORA	TORVALD
RANK	MORAL	HOPE	ACT	APPEARANCES

A Doll's House

SCENE	LAWS	LETTER	STAGE	KROGSTAD
FORGED	IBSEN	HELMER	APPEARANCES	ACT
HOPE	MORAL	FREE SPACE	TORVALD	NORA
LOAN	LINDE	BANK	BLACKMAIL	MOTHER
LOVE	JUSTICE	COPYING	PAPA	SUICIDE

A Doll's House

IBSEN	PAPA	LETTER	APPEARANCES	ITALY
LINDE	LOAN	HOPE	MOTHER	ACT
LAWS	CHILDREN	FREE SPACE	STAGE	HAPPINESS
LOVE	LARK	BANK	TORVALD	RANK
FORGED	BLACKMAIL	MORAL	SCENE	PROMOTION

A Doll's House

JUSTICE	NORA	HELMER	PEOPLE	DOLL
THIN	COPYING	SUICIDE	PROMOTION	SCENE
MORAL	BLACKMAIL	FREE SPACE	RANK	TORVALD
BANK	LARK	LOVE	HAPPINESS	STAGE
KROGSTAD	CHILDREN	LAWS	ACT	MOTHER

A Doll's House

LARK	LAWS	FORGED	HELMER	MORAL
STAGE	RANK	JUSTICE	PROMOTION	PAPA
MOTHER	BANK	FREE SPACE	HAPPINESS	DOLL
HOPE	ACT	NORA	TORVALD	LINDE
LETTER	PEOPLE	IBSEN	SUICIDE	THIN

A Doll's House

SCENE	BLACKMAIL	COPYING	APPEARANCES	ITALY
LOVE	KROGSTAD	CHILDREN	THIN	SUICIDE
IBSEN	PEOPLE	FREE SPACE	LINDE	TORVALD
NORA	ACT	HOPE	DOLL	HAPPINESS
LOAN	BANK	MOTHER	PAPA	PROMOTION

A Doll's House

TORVALD	ACT	NORA	MOTHER	PEOPLE
LETTER	HELMER	SCENE	RANK	BLACKMAIL
APPEARANCES	IBSEN	FREE SPACE	THIN	STAGE
PAPA	SUICIDE	HOPE	CHILDREN	FORGED
LARK	LOVE	COPYING	LINDE	HAPPINESS

A Doll's House

BANK	ITALY	MORAL	LOAN	JUSTICE
LAWS	KROGSTAD	PROMOTION	HAPPINESS	LINDE
COPYING	LOVE	FREE SPACE	FORGED	CHILDREN
HOPE	SUICIDE	PAPA	STAGE	THIN
DOLL	IBSEN	APPEARANCES	BLACKMAIL	RANK

A Doll's House

BANK	THIN	NORA	BLACKMAIL	ITALY
COPYING	APPEARANCES	LARK	FORGED	HAPPINESS
STAGE	TORVALD	FREE SPACE	LAWS	SCENE
PEOPLE	LOAN	MOTHER	DOLL	KROGSTAD
LINDE	HELMER	PROMOTION	IBSEN	JUSTICE

A Doll's House

SUICIDE	LETTER	CHILDREN	ACT	RANK
LOVE	HOPE	MORAL	JUSTICE	IBSEN
PROMOTION	HELMER	FREE SPACE	KROGSTAD	DOLL
MOTHER	LOAN	PEOPLE	SCENE	LAWS
PAPA	TORVALD	STAGE	HAPPINESS	FORGED

A Doll's House

CHILDREN	FORGED	HAPPINESS	SUICIDE	JUSTICE
LOVE	PAPA	BANK	HOPE	MOTHER
MORAL	SCENE	FREE SPACE	DOLL	COPYING
LARK	LAWS	TORVALD	APPEARANCES	HELMER
LETTER	LOAN	PEOPLE	NORA	ITALY

A Doll's House

RANK	BLACKMAIL	ACT	IBSEN	LINDE
PROMOTION	KROGSTAD	STAGE	ITALY	NORA
PEOPLE	LOAN	FREE SPACE	HELMER	APPEARANCES
TORVALD	LAWS	LARK	COPYING	DOLL
THIN	SCENE	MORAL	MOTHER	HOPE

A Doll's House

HOPE	PAPA	BLACKMAIL	LAWS	NORA
SUICIDE	CHILDREN	LARK	SCENE	LINDE
IBSEN	ITALY	FREE SPACE	STAGE	ACT
APPEARANCES	RANK	JUSTICE	PEOPLE	KROGSTAD
MOTHER	TORVALD	MORAL	LOVE	COPYING

A Doll's House

THIN	DOLL	LETTER	FORGED	HAPPINESS
PROMOTION	HELMER	LOAN	COPYING	LOVE
MORAL	TORVALD	FREE SPACE	KROGSTAD	PEOPLE
JUSTICE	RANK	APPEARANCES	ACT	STAGE
BANK	ITALY	IBSEN	LINDE	SCENE

A Doll's House

HAPPINESS	LOVE	LAWS	MORAL	JUSTICE
ITALY	HELMER	MOTHER	IBSEN	LETTER
PROMOTION	LOAN	FREE SPACE	SCENE	FORGED
BANK	TORVALD	PAPA	RANK	LINDE
THIN	APPEARANCES	DOLL	COPYING	SUICIDE

A Doll's House

KROGSTAD	NORA	HOPE	BLACKMAIL	ACT
PEOPLE	LARK	STAGE	SUICIDE	COPYING
DOLL	APPEARANCES	FREE SPACE	LINDE	RANK
PAPA	TORVALD	BANK	FORGED	SCENE
CHILDREN	LOAN	PROMOTION	LETTER	IBSEN

A Doll's House

LOAN	IBSEN	BLACKMAIL	FORGED	SCENE
NORA	BANK	COPYING	HAPPINESS	ACT
LARK	LETTER	FREE SPACE	PEOPLE	LOVE
MORAL	DOLL	JUSTICE	CHILDREN	LAWS
ITALY	SUICIDE	RANK	HELMER	HOPE

A Doll's House

TORVALD	PROMOTION	STAGE	MOTHER	APPEARANCES
KROGSTAD	PAPA	THIN	HOPE	HELMER
RANK	SUICIDE	FREE SPACE	LAWS	CHILDREN
JUSTICE	DOLL	MORAL	LOVE	PEOPLE
LINDE	LETTER	LARK	ACT	HAPPINESS

A Doll's House

MORAL	DOLL	HELMER	RANK	THIN
APPEARANCES	LOVE	JUSTICE	LAWS	ACT
LINDE	LOAN	FREE SPACE	BLACKMAIL	MOTHER
FORGED	NORA	PROMOTION	SUICIDE	SCENE
STAGE	LARK	PEOPLE	CHILDREN	BANK

A Doll's House

HOPE	PAPA	ITALY	IBSEN	HAPPINESS
LETTER	KROGSTAD	COPYING	BANK	CHILDREN
PEOPLE	LARK	FREE SPACE	SCENE	SUICIDE
PROMOTION	NORA	FORGED	MOTHER	BLACKMAIL
TORVALD	LOAN	LINDE	ACT	LAWS

A Doll's House

FORGED	MOTHER	IBSEN	SCENE	APPEARANCES
SUICIDE	COPYING	HAPPINESS	BANK	JUSTICE
KROGSTAD	NORA	FREE SPACE	LARK	LOAN
DOLL	LETTER	PROMOTION	HELMER	ITALY
TORVALD	PAPA	MORAL	LINDE	LAWS

A Doll's House

BLACKMAIL	HOPE	LOVE	ACT	STAGE
THIN	CHILDREN	PEOPLE	LAWS	LINDE
MORAL	PAPA	FREE SPACE	ITALY	HELMER
PROMOTION	LETTER	DOLL	LOAN	LARK
RANK	NORA	KROGSTAD	JUSTICE	BANK

A Doll's House Vocabulary Word List

No.	Word	Clue/Definition
1.	AMORTIZATION	Prorating or spreading the repayment of debt over a period of time
2.	BEDRIDDEN	Confined to bed due to illness
3.	BLUNDERED	Moved clumsily or stupidly into
4.	CAPRICIOUS	Impulsive; whimsical; unpredictable
5.	CONTRABAND	Illegal goods
6.	DEGENERATE	Having declined from a former state
7.	DISREPUTABLE	Lacking respectability; shady
8.	DOMINO	Costume with a hooded robe
9.	EVASION	Act of avoiding
10.	EXCRUCIATING	Agonizing; painful
11.	FRIVOLOUS	Trivial; silly; unimportant
12.	HYPOCRITE	One who say he believes one way but whose actions show he believes the opposite
13.	HYSTERICS	Emotional outbursts
14.	INCOMPETENT	Lacking abilities
15.	INCREDULOUSLY	With disbelief
16.	INDISCREET	Lacking discretion; not judicious; unwise
17.	INTERFERED	Got in the way; hindered
18.	INTOLERABLE	Unbearable
19.	JAUNTILY	Briskly; full of self-confidence
20.	RAVISHING	Extremely attractive
21.	REFINEMENT	Having good manners and social graces
22.	REPROACH	Criticism
23.	RETRIBUTION	Justly deserved punishment
24.	SEIZING	Grabbing; taking & holding
25.	SQUANDERING	Wasting money on extravagant purchases
26.	STAVE	Hold off; keep away
27.	SUPPRESSING	Holding down or holding back
28.	TARANTELLA	Lively Italian dance
29.	TUMULTUOUS	Extremely noisy and disorderly
30.	UNPERTURBED	Unruffled; not bothered; calmly
31.	VEHEMENTLY	Forcefully; full of strong emotions

Copyrighted

A Doll's House Vocabulary Fill In The Blanks 1

_____ 1. Moved clumsily or stupidly into

_____ 2. Extremely noisy and disorderly

_____ 3. Emotional outbursts

_____ 4. Lacking abilities

_____ 5. Prorating or spreading the repayment of debt over a period of time

_____ 6. Lacking respectability; shady

_____ 7. Got in the way; hindered

_____ 8. Trivial; silly; unimportant

_____ 9. Grabbing; taking & holding

_____ 10. Lacking discretion; not judicious; unwise

_____ 11. With disbelief

_____ 12. Wasting money on extravagant purchases

_____ 13. Forcefully; full of strong emotions

_____ 14. Justly deserved punishment

_____ 15. Confined to bed due to illness

_____ 16. Act of avoiding

_____ 17. Holding down or holding back

_____ 18. Unruffled; not bothered; calmly

_____ 19. Hold off; keep away

_____ 20. Criticism

A Doll's House Vocabulary Fill In The Blanks 1 Answer Key

BLUNDERED	1. Moved clumsily or stupidly into
TUMULTUOUS	2. Extremely noisy and disorderly
HYSTERICS	3. Emotional outbursts
INCOMPETENT	4. Lacking abilities
AMORTIZATION	5. Prorating or spreading the repayment of debt over a period of time
DISREPUTABLE	6. Lacking respectability; shady
INTERFERED	7. Got in the way; hindered
FRIVOLOUS	8. Trivial; silly; unimportant
SEIZING	9. Grabbing; taking & holding
INDISCREET	10. Lacking discretion; not judicious; unwise
INCREDULOUSLY	11. With disbelief
SQUANDERING	12. Wasting money on extravagant purchases
VEHEMENTLY	13. Forcefully; full of strong emotions
RETRIBUTION	14. Justly deserved punishment
BEDRIDDEN	15. Confined to bed due to illness
EVASION	16. Act of avoiding
SUPPRESSING	17. Holding down or holding back
UNPERTURBED	18. Unruffled; not bothered; calmly
STAVE	19. Hold off; keep away
REPROACH	20. Criticism

A Doll's House Vocabulary Fill In The Blanks 2

_____ 1. Unbearable

_____ 2. Confined to bed due to illness

_____ 3. Unruffled; not bothered; calmly

_____ 4. Lacking abilities

_____ 5. Forcefully; full of strong emotions

_____ 6. Moved clumsily or stupidly into

_____ 7. Having good manners and social graces

_____ 8. Agonizing; painful

_____ 9. Prorating or spreading the repayment of debt over a period of time

_____ 10. Grabbing; taking & holding

_____ 11. Lacking respectability; shady

_____ 12. Trivial; silly; unimportant

_____ 13. One who say he believes one way but whose actions show he believes the opposite

_____ 14. Hold off; keep away

_____ 15. With disbelief

_____ 16. Briskly; full of self-confidence

_____ 17. Having declined from a former state

_____ 18. Costume with a hooded robe

_____ 19. Wasting money on extravagant purchases

_____ 20. Holding down or holding back

A Doll's House Vocabulary Fill In The Blanks 2 Answer Key

INTOLERABLE	1. Unbearable
BEDRIDDEN	2. Confined to bed due to illness
UNPERTURBED	3. Unruffled; not bothered; calmly
INCOMPETENT	4. Lacking abilities
VEHEMENTLY	5. Forcefully; full of strong emotions
BLUNDERED	6. Moved clumsily or stupidly into
REFINEMENT	7. Having good manners and social graces
EXCRUCIATING	8. Agonizing; painful
AMORTIZATION	9. Prorating or spreading the repayment of debt over a period of time
SEIZING	10. Grabbing; taking & holding
DISREPUTABLE	11. Lacking respectability; shady
FRIVOLOUS	12. Trivial; silly; unimportant
HYPOCRITE	13. One who say he believes one way but whose actions show he believes the opposite
STAVE	14. Hold off; keep away
INCREDULOUSLY	15. With disbelief
JAUNTILY	16. Briskly; full of self-confidence
DEGENERATE	17. Having declined from a former state
DOMINO	18. Costume with a hooded robe
SQUANDERING	19. Wasting money on extravagant purchases
SUPPRESSING	20. Holding down or holding back

A Doll's House Vocabulary Fill In The Blanks 3

1. Lively Italian dance
2. Unruffled; not bothered; calmly
3. Impulsive; whimsical; unpredictable
4. Forcefully; full of strong emotions
5. Trivial; silly; unimportant
6. Wasting money on extravagant purchases
7. Criticism
8. Extremely noisy and disorderly
9. Having good manners and social graces
10. Moved clumsily or stupidly into
11. Lacking abilities
12. Act of avoiding
13. Holding down or holding back
14. Emotional outbursts
15. One who say he believes one way but whose actions show he believes the opposite
16. Confined to bed due to illness
17. Agonizing; painful
18. Hold off; keep away
19. Extremely attractive
20. Having declined from a former state

A Doll's House Vocabulary Fill In The Blanks 3 Answer Key

TARANTELLA	1. Lively Italian dance
UNPERTURBED	2. Unruffled; not bothered; calmly
CAPRICIOUS	3. Impulsive; whimsical; unpredictable
VEHEMENTLY	4. Forcefully; full of strong emotions
FRIVOLOUS	5. Trivial; silly; unimportant
SQUANDERING	6. Wasting money on extravagant purchases
REPROACH	7. Criticism
TUMULTUOUS	8. Extremely noisy and disorderly
REFINEMENT	9. Having good manners and social graces
BLUNDERED	10. Moved clumsily or stupidly into
INCOMPETENT	11. Lacking abilities
EVASION	12. Act of avoiding
SUPPRESSING	13. Holding down or holding back
HYSTERICS	14. Emotional outbursts
HYPOCRITE	15. One who say he believes one way but whose actions show he believes the opposite
BEDRIDDEN	16. Confined to bed due to illness
EXCRUCIATING	17. Agonizing; painful
STAVE	18. Hold off; keep away
RAVISHING	19. Extremely attractive
DEGENERATE	20. Having declined from a former state

A Doll's House Vocabulary Fill In The Blanks 4

_____ 1. Forcefully; full of strong emotions

_____ 2. Criticism

_____ 3. Having declined from a former state

_____ 4. Wasting money on extravagant purchases

_____ 5. Lacking discretion; not judicious; unwise

_____ 6. With disbelief

_____ 7. Lacking abilities

_____ 8. Lacking respectability; shady

_____ 9. Holding down or holding back

_____ 10. Extremely attractive

_____ 11. Emotional outbursts

_____ 12. Justly deserved punishment

_____ 13. Impulsive; whimsical; unpredictable

_____ 14. Illegal goods

_____ 15. Costume with a hooded robe

_____ 16. Trivial; silly; unimportant

_____ 17. Grabbing; taking & holding

_____ 18. Got in the way; hindered

_____ 19. Unruffled; not bothered; calmly

_____ 20. Having good manners and social graces

A Doll's House Vocabulary Fill In The Blanks 4 Answer Key

VEHEMENTLY	1. Forcefully; full of strong emotions
REPROACH	2. Criticism
DEGENERATE	3. Having declined from a former state
SQUANDERING	4. Wasting money on extravagant purchases
INDISCREET	5. Lacking discretion; not judicious; unwise
INCREDULOUSLY	6. With disbelief
INCOMPETENT	7. Lacking abilities
DISREPUTABLE	8. Lacking respectability; shady
SUPPRESSING	9. Holding down or holding back
RAVISHING	10. Extremely attractive
HYSTERICS	11. Emotional outbursts
RETRIBUTION	12. Justly deserved punishment
CAPRICIOUS	13. Impulsive; whimsical; unpredictable
CONTRABAND	14. Illegal goods
DOMINO	15. Costume with a hooded robe
FRIVOLOUS	16. Trivial; silly; unimportant
SEIZING	17. Grabbing; taking & holding
INTERFERED	18. Got in the way; hindered
UNPERTURBED	19. Unruffled; not bothered; calmly
REFINEMENT	20. Having good manners and social graces

A Doll's House Vocabulary Matching 1

___ 1. STAVE
___ 2. BLUNDERED
___ 3. SEIZING
___ 4. FRIVOLOUS
___ 5. SUPPRESSING
___ 6. TUMULTUOUS
___ 7. BEDRIDDEN
___ 8. RETRIBUTION
___ 9. TARANTELLA
___ 10. SQUANDERING
___ 11. HYPOCRITE
___ 12. INTERFERED
___ 13. EXCRUCIATING
___ 14. UNPERTURBED
___ 15. EVASION
___ 16. DISREPUTABLE
___ 17. JAUNTILY
___ 18. DEGENERATE
___ 19. INCOMPETENT
___ 20. RAVISHING
___ 21. REFINEMENT
___ 22. AMORTIZATION
___ 23. CAPRICIOUS
___ 24. HYSTERICS
___ 25. CONTRABAND

A. Holding down or holding back
B. Justly deserved punishment
C. Extremely attractive
D. Unruffled; not bothered; calmly
E. Having good manners and social graces
F. Prorating or spreading the repayment of debt over a period of time
G. Lacking abilities
H. Trivial; silly; unimportant
I. One who say he believes one way but whose actions show he believes the opposite
J. Hold off; keep away
K. Act of avoiding
L. Extremely noisy and disorderly
M. Confined to bed due to illness
N. Moved clumsily or stupidly into
O. Got in the way; hindered
P. Lively Italian dance
Q. Agonizing; painful
R. Briskly; full of self-confidence
S. Impulsive; whimsical; unpredictable
T. Illegal goods
U. Grabbing; taking & holding
V. Lacking respectability; shady
W. Wasting money on extravagant purchases
X. Having declined from a former state
Y. Emotional outbursts

A Doll's House Vocabulary Matching 1 Answer Key

J - 1. STAVE	A.	Holding down or holding back
N - 2. BLUNDERED	B.	Justly deserved punishment
U - 3. SEIZING	C.	Extremely attractive
H - 4. FRIVOLOUS	D.	Unruffled; not bothered; calmly
A - 5. SUPPRESSING	E.	Having good manners and social graces
L - 6. TUMULTUOUS	F.	Prorating or spreading the repayment of debt over a period of time
M - 7. BEDRIDDEN	G.	Lacking abilities
B - 8. RETRIBUTION	H.	Trivial; silly; unimportant
P - 9. TARANTELLA	I.	One who say he believes one way but whose actions show he believes the opposite
W - 10. SQUANDERING	J.	Hold off; keep away
I - 11. HYPOCRITE	K.	Act of avoiding
O - 12. INTERFERED	L.	Extremely noisy and disorderly
Q - 13. EXCRUCIATING	M.	Confined to bed due to illness
D - 14. UNPERTURBED	N.	Moved clumsily or stupidly into
K - 15. EVASION	O.	Got in the way; hindered
V - 16. DISREPUTABLE	P.	Lively Italian dance
R - 17. JAUNTILY	Q.	Agonizing; painful
X - 18. DEGENERATE	R.	Briskly; full of self-confidence
G - 19. INCOMPETENT	S.	Impulsive; whimsical; unpredictable
C - 20. RAVISHING	T.	Illegal goods
E - 21. REFINEMENT	U.	Grabbing; taking & holding
F - 22. AMORTIZATION	V.	Lacking respectability; shady
S - 23. CAPRICIOUS	W.	Wasting money on extravagant purchases
Y - 24. HYSTERICS	X.	Having declined from a former state
T - 25. CONTRABAND	Y.	Emotional outbursts

A Doll's House Vocabulary Matching 2

___ 1. HYSTERICS
___ 2. DEGENERATE
___ 3. TUMULTUOUS
___ 4. TARANTELLA
___ 5. EXCRUCIATING
___ 6. CONTRABAND
___ 7. EVASION
___ 8. INCREDULOUSLY
___ 9. SEIZING
___ 10. UNPERTURBED
___ 11. HYPOCRITE
___ 12. DOMINO
___ 13. VEHEMENTLY
___ 14. FRIVOLOUS
___ 15. RETRIBUTION
___ 16. CAPRICIOUS
___ 17. INDISCREET
___ 18. BEDRIDDEN
___ 19. SUPPRESSING
___ 20. STAVE
___ 21. RAVISHING
___ 22. BLUNDERED
___ 23. DISREPUTABLE
___ 24. AMORTIZATION
___ 25. REFINEMENT

A. Justly deserved punishment
B. Lacking discretion; not judicious; unwise
C. Hold off; keep away
D. Lacking respectability; shady
E. Having good manners and social graces
F. Lively Italian dance
G. Confined to bed due to illness
H. Impulsive; whimsical; unpredictable
I. Agonizing; painful
J. Extremely attractive
K. Prorating or spreading the repayment of debt over a period of time
L. Moved clumsily or stupidly into
M. Costume with a hooded robe
N. Extremely noisy and disorderly
O. Illegal goods
P. Unruffled; not bothered; calmly
Q. Grabbing; taking & holding
R. Act of avoiding
S. Holding down or holding back
T. Trivial; silly; unimportant
U. Having declined from a former state
V. One who say he believes one way but whose actions show he believes the opposite
W. With disbelief
X. Forcefully; full of strong emotions
Y. Emotional outbursts

A Doll's House Vocabulary Matching 2 Answer Key

Y - 1. HYSTERICS
U - 2. DEGENERATE
N - 3. TUMULTUOUS
F - 4. TARANTELLA
I - 5. EXCRUCIATING
O - 6. CONTRABAND
R - 7. EVASION
W - 8. INCREDULOUSLY
Q - 9. SEIZING
P - 10. UNPERTURBED
V - 11. HYPOCRITE
M - 12. DOMINO
X - 13. VEHEMENTLY
T - 14. FRIVOLOUS
A - 15. RETRIBUTION
H - 16. CAPRICIOUS
B - 17. INDISCREET
G - 18. BEDRIDDEN
S - 19. SUPPRESSING
C - 20. STAVE
J - 21. RAVISHING
L - 22. BLUNDERED
D - 23. DISREPUTABLE
K - 24. AMORTIZATION
E - 25. REFINEMENT

A. Justly deserved punishment
B. Lacking discretion; not judicious; unwise
C. Hold off; keep away
D. Lacking respectability; shady
E. Having good manners and social graces
F. Lively Italian dance
G. Confined to bed due to illness
H. Impulsive; whimsical; unpredictable
I. Agonizing; painful
J. Extremely attractive
K. Prorating or spreading the repayment of debt over a period of time
L. Moved clumsily or stupidly into
M. Costume with a hooded robe
N. Extremely noisy and disorderly
O. Illegal goods
P. Unruffled; not bothered; calmly
Q. Grabbing; taking & holding
R. Act of avoiding
S. Holding down or holding back
T. Trivial; silly; unimportant
U. Having declined from a former state
V. One who say he believes one way but whose actions show he believes the opposite
W. With disbelief
X. Forcefully; full of strong emotions
Y. Emotional outbursts

A Doll's House Vocabulary Matching 3

___ 1. TUMULTUOUS   A. Got in the way; hindered
___ 2. REFINEMENT   B. Agonizing; painful
___ 3. VEHEMENTLY   C. Moved clumsily or stupidly into
___ 4. INTERFERED   D. Hold off; keep away
___ 5. DEGENERATE   E. Lively Italian dance
___ 6. RAVISHING   F. Illegal goods
___ 7. STAVE   G. Justly deserved punishment
___ 8. INCOMPETENT   H. Confined to bed due to illness
___ 9. RETRIBUTION   I. Trivial; silly; unimportant
___10. SEIZING   J. Forcefully; full of strong emotions
___11. SQUANDERING   K. Holding down or holding back
___12. EXCRUCIATING   L. Prorating or spreading the repayment of debt over a period of time
___13. BLUNDERED   M. Extremely attractive
___14. SUPPRESSING   N. Criticism
___15. CONTRABAND   O. Lacking discretion; not judicious; unwise
___16. REPROACH   P. Extremely noisy and disorderly
___17. TARANTELLA   Q. Having declined from a former state
___18. HYPOCRITE   R. One who say he believes one way but whose actions show he believes the opposite
___19. BEDRIDDEN   S. Wasting money on extravagant purchases
___20. JAUNTILY   T. Grabbing; taking & holding
___21. AMORTIZATION   U. Unbearable
___22. EVASION   V. Act of avoiding
___23. INTOLERABLE   W. Briskly; full of self-confidence
___24. FRIVOLOUS   X. Lacking abilities
___25. INDISCREET   Y. Having good manners and social graces

A Doll's House Vocabulary Matching 3 Answer Key

P - 1.	TUMULTUOUS	A. Got in the way; hindered
Y - 2.	REFINEMENT	B. Agonizing; painful
J - 3.	VEHEMENTLY	C. Moved clumsily or stupidly into
A - 4.	INTERFERED	D. Hold off; keep away
Q - 5.	DEGENERATE	E. Lively Italian dance
M - 6.	RAVISHING	F. Illegal goods
D - 7.	STAVE	G. Justly deserved punishment
X - 8.	INCOMPETENT	H. Confined to bed due to illness
G - 9.	RETRIBUTION	I. Trivial; silly; unimportant
T - 10.	SEIZING	J. Forcefully; full of strong emotions
S - 11.	SQUANDERING	K. Holding down or holding back
B - 12.	EXCRUCIATING	L. Prorating or spreading the repayment of debt over a period of time
C - 13.	BLUNDERED	M. Extremely attractive
K - 14.	SUPPRESSING	N. Criticism
F - 15.	CONTRABAND	O. Lacking discretion; not judicious; unwise
N - 16.	REPROACH	P. Extremely noisy and disorderly
E - 17.	TARANTELLA	Q. Having declined from a former state
R - 18.	HYPOCRITE	R. One who say he believes one way but whose actions show he believes the opposite
H - 19.	BEDRIDDEN	S. Wasting money on extravagant purchases
W - 20.	JAUNTILY	T. Grabbing; taking & holding
L - 21.	AMORTIZATION	U. Unbearable
V - 22.	EVASION	V. Act of avoiding
U - 23.	INTOLERABLE	W. Briskly; full of self-confidence
I - 24.	FRIVOLOUS	X. Lacking abilities
O - 25.	INDISCREET	Y. Having good manners and social graces

A Doll's House Vocabulary Matching 4

___ 1. CONTRABAND   A. Grabbing; taking & holding
___ 2. AMORTIZATION   B. Lacking respectability; shady
___ 3. INTOLERABLE   C. Unruffled; not bothered; calmly
___ 4. SQUANDERING   D. Lively Italian dance
___ 5. FRIVOLOUS   E. Unbearable
___ 6. STAVE   F. Emotional outbursts
___ 7. JAUNTILY   G. Costume with a hooded robe
___ 8. TARANTELLA   H. One who say he believes one way but whose actions show he believes the opposite
___ 9. SUPPRESSING   I. With disbelief
___10. HYPOCRITE   J. Hold off; keep away
___11. DISREPUTABLE   K. Act of avoiding
___12. SEIZING   L. Criticism
___13. RETRIBUTION   M. Wasting money on extravagant purchases
___14. CAPRICIOUS   N. Illegal goods
___15. VEHEMENTLY   O. Got in the way; hindered
___16. INCREDULOUSLY   P. Prorating or spreading the repayment of debt over a period of time
___17. REPROACH   Q. Justly deserved punishment
___18. UNPERTURBED   R. Lacking discretion; not judicious; unwise
___19. INCOMPETENT   S. Forcefully; full of strong emotions
___20. HYSTERICS   T. Impulsive; whimsical; unpredictable
___21. DOMINO   U. Holding down or holding back
___22. EVASION   V. Briskly; full of self-confidence
___23. INTERFERED   W. Trivial; silly; unimportant
___24. INDISCREET   X. Having good manners and social graces
___25. REFINEMENT   Y. Lacking abilities

A Doll's House Vocabulary Matching 4 Answer Key

- N - 1. CONTRABAND
- P - 2. AMORTIZATION
- E - 3. INTOLERABLE
- M - 4. SQUANDERING
- W - 5. FRIVOLOUS
- J - 6. STAVE
- V - 7. JAUNTILY
- D - 8. TARANTELLA
- U - 9. SUPPRESSING
- H - 10. HYPOCRITE
- B - 11. DISREPUTABLE
- A - 12. SEIZING
- Q - 13. RETRIBUTION
- T - 14. CAPRICIOUS
- S - 15. VEHEMENTLY
- I - 16. INCREDULOUSLY
- L - 17. REPROACH
- C - 18. UNPERTURBED
- Y - 19. INCOMPETENT
- F - 20. HYSTERICS
- G - 21. DOMINO
- K - 22. EVASION
- O - 23. INTERFERED
- R - 24. INDISCREET
- X - 25. REFINEMENT

A. Grabbing; taking & holding
B. Lacking respectability; shady
C. Unruffled; not bothered; calmly
D. Lively Italian dance
E. Unbearable
F. Emotional outbursts
G. Costume with a hooded robe
H. One who say he believes one way but whose actions show he believes the opposite
I. With disbelief
J. Hold off; keep away
K. Act of avoiding
L. Criticism
M. Wasting money on extravagant purchases
N. Illegal goods
O. Got in the way; hindered
P. Prorating or spreading the repayment of debt over a period of time
Q. Justly deserved punishment
R. Lacking discretion; not judicious; unwise
S. Forcefully; full of strong emotions
T. Impulsive; whimsical; unpredictable
U. Holding down or holding back
V. Briskly; full of self-confidence
W. Trivial; silly; unimportant
X. Having good manners and social graces
Y. Lacking abilities

A Doll's House Vocabulary Magic Squares 1

Match the definition with the vocabulary word. Put your answers in the magic squares below. When your answers are correct, all columns and rows will add to the same number.

A. UNPERTURBED
B. AMORTIZATION
C. TUMULTUOUS
D. INCREDULOUSLY
E. DEGENERATE
F. INDISCREET
G. CAPRICIOUS
H. SEIZING
I. HYPOCRITE
J. INTOLERABLE
K. INCOMPETENT
L. BEDRIDDEN
M. INTERFERED
N. REFINEMENT
O. EVASION
P. JAUNTILY

1. Grabbing; taking & holding
2. Got in the way; hindered
3. Prorating or spreading the repayment of debt over a period of time
4. Lacking abilities
5. Unbearable
6. Extremely noisy and disorderly
7. Briskly; full of self-confidence
8. Having declined from a former state
9. Act of avoiding
10. Lacking discretion; not judicious; unwise
11. One who say he believes one way but whose actions show he believes the opposite
12. With disbelief
13. Unruffled; not bothered; calmly
14. Confined to bed due to illness
15. Impulsive; whimsical; unpredictable
16. Having good manners and social graces

A=	B=	C=	D=
E=	F=	G=	H=
I=	J=	K=	L=
M=	N=	O=	P=

A Doll's House Vocabulary Magic Squares 1 Answer Key

Match the definition with the vocabulary word. Put your answers in the magic squares below. When your answers are correct, all columns and rows will add to the same number.

A. UNPERTURBED
B. AMORTIZATION
C. TUMULTUOUS
D. INCREDULOUSLY
E. DEGENERATE
F. INDISCREET
G. CAPRICIOUS
H. SEIZING
I. HYPOCRITE
J. INTOLERABLE
K. INCOMPETENT
L. BEDRIDDEN
M. INTERFERED
N. REFINEMENT
O. EVASION
P. JAUNTILY

1. Grabbing; taking & holding
2. Got in the way; hindered
3. Prorating or spreading the repayment of debt over a period of time
4. Lacking abilities
5. Unbearable
6. Extremely noisy and disorderly
7. Briskly; full of self-confidence
8. Having declined from a former state
9. Act of avoiding
10. Lacking discretion; not judicious; unwise
11. One who say he believes one way but whose actions show he believes the opposite
12. With disbelief
13. Unruffled; not bothered; calmly
14. Confined to bed due to illness
15. Impulsive; whimsical; unpredictable
16. Having good manners and social graces

A=13	B=3	C=6	D=12
E=8	F=10	G=15	H=1
I=11	J=5	K=4	L=14
M=2	N=16	O=9	P=7

A Doll's House Vocabulary Magic Squares 2

Match the definition with the vocabulary word. Put your answers in the magic squares below. When your answers are correct, all columns and rows will add to the same number.

A. JAUNTILY
B. INCREDULOUSLY
C. HYPOCRITE
D. REPROACH
E. REFINEMENT
F. SEIZING
G. DOMINO
H. DEGENERATE
I. SUPPRESSING
J. TARANTELLA
K. EVASION
L. INTOLERABLE
M. RETRIBUTION
N. HYSTERICS
O. BLUNDERED
P. UNPERTURBED

1. One who say he believes one way but whose actions show he believes the opposite
2. Lively Italian dance
3. Grabbing; taking & holding
4. Moved clumsily or stupidly into
5. Unruffled; not bothered; calmly
6. Having good manners and social graces
7. Holding down or holding back
8. Criticism
9. Justly deserved punishment
10. Having declined from a former state
11. Unbearable
12. Briskly; full of self-confidence
13. With disbelief
14. Act of avoiding
15. Costume with a hooded robe
16. Emotional outbursts

A=	B=	C=	D=
E=	F=	G=	H=
I=	J=	K=	L=
M=	N=	O=	P=

A Doll's House Vocabulary Magic Squares 2 Answer Key

Match the definition with the vocabulary word. Put your answers in the magic squares below. When your answers are correct, all columns and rows will add to the same number.

A. JAUNTILY
B. INCREDULOUSLY
C. HYPOCRITE
D. REPROACH
E. REFINEMENT
F. SEIZING
G. DOMINO
H. DEGENERATE
I. SUPPRESSING
J. TARANTELLA
K. EVASION
L. INTOLERABLE
M. RETRIBUTION
N. HYSTERICS
O. BLUNDERED
P. UNPERTURBED

1. One who say he believes one way but whose actions show he believes the opposite
2. Lively Italian dance
3. Grabbing; taking & holding
4. Moved clumsily or stupidly into
5. Unruffled; not bothered; calmly
6. Having good manners and social graces
7. Holding down or holding back
8. Criticism
9. Justly deserved punishment
10. Having declined from a former state
11. Unbearable
12. Briskly; full of self-confidence
13. With disbelief
14. Act of avoiding
15. Costume with a hooded robe
16. Emotional outbursts

A=12	B=13	C=1	D=8
E=6	F=3	G=15	H=10
I=7	J=2	K=14	L=11
M=9	N=16	O=4	P=5

A Doll's House Vocabulary Magic Squares 3

Match the definition with the vocabulary word. Put your answers in the magic squares below. When your answers are correct, all columns and rows will add to the same number.

A. CAPRICIOUS
B. EXCRUCIATING
C. DISREPUTABLE
D. SEIZING
E. RAVISHING
F. INCOMPETENT
G. INDISCREET
H. TARANTELLA
I. EVASION
J. SUPPRESSING
K. HYSTERICS
L. FRIVOLOUS
M. SQUANDERING
N. UNPERTURBED
O. BLUNDERED
P. TUMULTUOUS

1. Wasting money on extravagant purchases
2. Lacking abilities
3. Lively Italian dance
4. Moved clumsily or stupidly into
5. Trivial; silly; unimportant
6. Lacking respectability; shady
7. Impulsive; whimsical; unpredictable
8. Holding down or holding back
9. Emotional outbursts
10. Grabbing; taking & holding
11. Agonizing; painful
12. Act of avoiding
13. Unruffled; not bothered; calmly
14. Extremely attractive
15. Lacking discretion; not judicious; unwise
16. Extremely noisy and disorderly

A=	B=	C=	D=
E=	F=	G=	H=
I=	J=	K=	L=
M=	N=	O=	P=

A Doll's House Vocabulary Magic Squares 3 Answer Key

Match the definition with the vocabulary word. Put your answers in the magic squares below. When your answers are correct, all columns and rows will add to the same number.

A. CAPRICIOUS
B. EXCRUCIATING
C. DISREPUTABLE
D. SEIZING
E. RAVISHING
F. INCOMPETENT
G. INDISCREET
H. TARANTELLA
I. EVASION
J. SUPPRESSING
K. HYSTERICS
L. FRIVOLOUS
M. SQUANDERING
N. UNPERTURBED
O. BLUNDERED
P. TUMULTUOUS

1. Wasting money on extravagant purchases
2. Lacking abilities
3. Lively Italian dance
4. Moved clumsily or stupidly into
5. Trivial; silly; unimportant
6. Lacking respectability; shady
7. Impulsive; whimsical; unpredictable
8. Holding down or holding back
9. Emotional outbursts
10. Grabbing; taking & holding
11. Agonizing; painful
12. Act of avoiding
13. Unruffled; not bothered; calmly
14. Extremely attractive
15. Lacking discretion; not judicious; unwise
16. Extremely noisy and disorderly

A=7	B=11	C=6	D=10
E=14	F=2	G=15	H=3
I=12	J=8	K=9	L=5
M=1	N=13	O=4	P=16

A Doll's House Vocabulary Magic Squares 4

Match the definition with the vocabulary word. Put your answers in the magic squares below. When your answers are correct, all columns and rows will add to the same number.

A. INDISCREET
B. DISREPUTABLE
C. REFINEMENT
D. DEGENERATE
E. TUMULTUOUS
F. INCOMPETENT
G. HYSTERICS
H. INTERFERED
I. STAVE
J. SEIZING
K. CONTRABAND
L. JAUNTILY
M. AMORTIZATION
N. DOMINO
O. VEHEMENTLY
P. BEDRIDDEN

1. Got in the way; hindered
2. Lacking discretion; not judicious; unwise
3. Lacking respectability; shady
4. Emotional outbursts
5. Grabbing; taking & holding
6. Forcefully; full of strong emotions
7. Confined to bed due to illness
8. Hold off; keep away
9. Illegal goods
10. Costume with a hooded robe
11. Prorating or spreading the repayment of debt over a period of time
12. Briskly; full of self-confidence
13. Extremely noisy and disorderly
14. Having declined from a former state
15. Having good manners and social graces
16. Lacking abilities

A=	B=	C=	D=
E=	F=	G=	H=
I=	J=	K=	L=
M=	N=	O=	P=

A Doll's House Vocabulary Magic Squares 4 Answer Key

Match the definition with the vocabulary word. Put your answers in the magic squares below. When your answers are correct, all columns and rows will add to the same number.

A. INDISCREET
B. DISREPUTABLE
C. REFINEMENT
D. DEGENERATE
E. TUMULTUOUS
F. INCOMPETENT
G. HYSTERICS
H. INTERFERED
I. STAVE
J. SEIZING
K. CONTRABAND
L. JAUNTILY
M. AMORTIZATION
N. DOMINO
O. VEHEMENTLY
P. BEDRIDDEN

1. Got in the way; hindered
2. Lacking discretion; not judicious; unwise
3. Lacking respectability; shady
4. Emotional outbursts
5. Grabbing; taking & holding
6. Forcefully; full of strong emotions
7. Confined to bed due to illness
8. Hold off; keep away
9. Illegal goods
10. Costume with a hooded robe
11. Prorating or spreading the repayment of debt over a period of time
12. Briskly; full of self-confidence
13. Extremely noisy and disorderly
14. Having declined from a former state
15. Having good manners and social graces
16. Lacking abilities

A=2	B=3	C=15	D=14
E=13	F=16	G=4	H=1
I=8	J=5	K=9	L=12
M=11	N=10	O=6	P=7

A Doll's House Vocabulary Word Search 1

Words are placed backwards, forward, diagonally, up and down. Clues listed below can help you find the words. Circle the hidden vocabulary words in the maze.

```
D H D I S R E P U T A B L E P G I C P V R
E R Y C N P X M B Z G M C Q X N O Q Y L
G C E P C T K X L C Q T S B D I C N D J M
E J Q F O X E Q N K R Y Q I S R R T Y G R
N S U O I C I R P A C X S V U E R T N T
E K J N B N R B F C W C R E P D D A Z I X
R V W O B E E I Q E R C M H P N U B H T Z
A Q N I B F D M T E R K C E R A L A E A C
T N T T N F P R E E K Q M E U O N L I Z
E S A U X F R T I N W D E S Q U D B C Z
Z Q M B M H S B X D T F R N S S H A U S
P D O I Z U G R X D J W T I T L B R R Q
B H R R Z L B G B E R N Y G L N Y O E C K
T G T T L W Z T D R X N Y G T N P L X K
M I I E J K Y R U J N A V C L I R E O E J
M N Z R Y M B G Z O W H M O V C T S Y
G C A P N H Y P P L U I Y O A A C X N L H
H O T F R I V O L L O U S D C S E I Z I N G
K M I V T K V E T F T H I B R H T M L W
R P O H Z B T M W E M I O G Z B N B C K X
V E N L F N L L R G X N P S Q U N C L X D
V T S T A V L I R R G H G F T A P Y B R J L
Y E X R J V C V W H B R F J C D V P J Y G
N N A W Q S M N J Q H J K J C J J B S S
M T U N P E R T U R B E D E R E D N U L B
```

Act of avoiding (7)
Agonizing; painful (12)
Briskly; full of self-confidence (8)
Confined to bed due to illness (9)
Costume with a hooded robe (6)
Criticism (8)
Emotional outbursts (9)
Extremely attractive (9)
Extremely noisy and disorderly (10)
Forcefully; full of strong emotions (10)
Got in the way; hindered (10)
Grabbing; taking & holding (7)
Having declined from a former state (10)
Having good manners and social graces (10)
Hold off; keep away (5)
Holding down or holding back (11)
Illegal goods (10)
Impulsive; whimsical; unpredictable (10)
Justly deserved punishment (11)
Lacking abilities (11)
Lacking discretion; not judicious; unwise (10)

Lacking respectability; shady (12)
Lively Italian dance (10)
Moved clumsily or stupidly into (9)
One who say he believes one way but whose actions show he believes the opposite (9)
Prorating or spreading the repayment of debt over a period of time (12)
Trivial; silly; unimportant (9)
Unbearable (11)
Unruffled; not bothered; calmly (11)
Wasting money on extravagant purchases (11)
With disbelief (13)

A Doll's House Vocabulary Word Search 1 Answer Key

Words are placed backwards, forward, diagonally, up and down. Clues listed below can help you find the words. Circle the hidden vocabulary words in the maze.

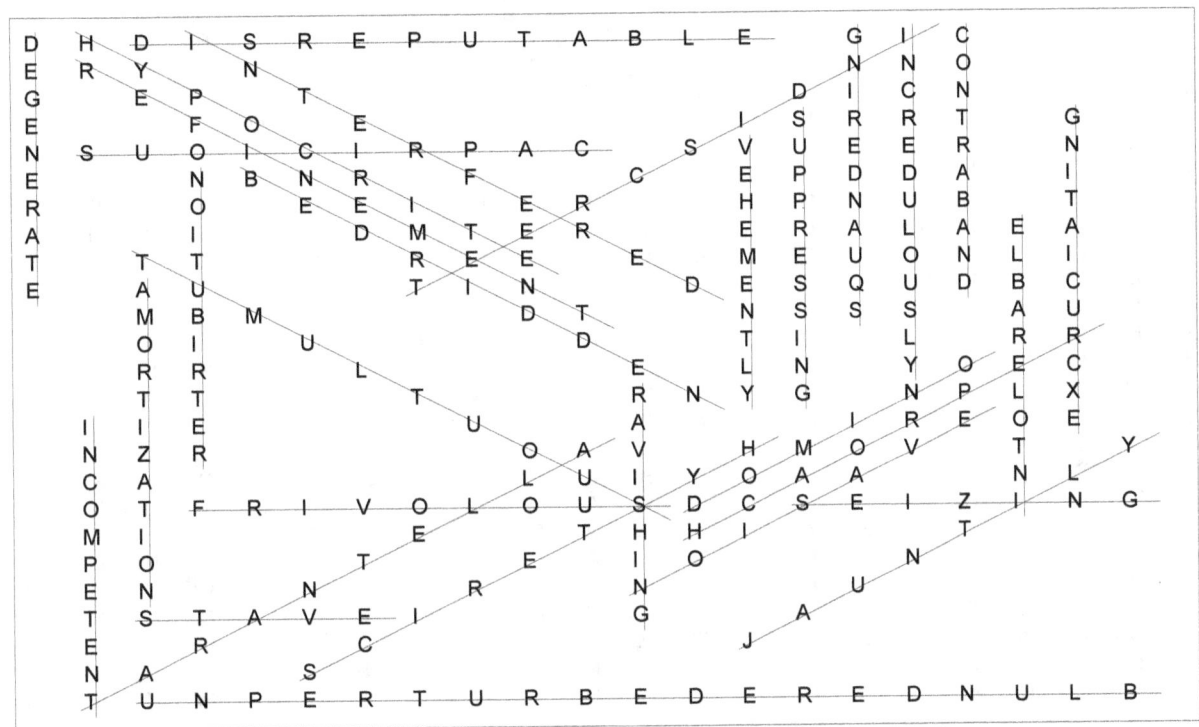

Act of avoiding (7)
Agonizing; painful (12)
Briskly; full of self-confidence (8)
Confined to bed due to illness (9)
Costume with a hooded robe (6)
Criticism (8)
Emotional outbursts (9)
Extremely attractive (9)
Extremely noisy and disorderly (10)
Forcefully; full of strong emotions (10)
Got in the way; hindered (10)
Grabbing; taking & holding (7)
Having declined from a former state (10)
Having good manners and social graces (10)
Hold off; keep away (5)
Holding down or holding back (11)
Illegal goods (10)
Impulsive; whimsical; unpredictable (10)
Justly deserved punishment (11)
Lacking abilities (11)
Lacking discretion; not judicious; unwise (10)

Lacking respectability; shady (12)
Lively Italian dance (10)
Moved clumsily or stupidly into (9)
One who say he believes one way but whose actions show he believes the opposite (9)
Prorating or spreading the repayment of debt over a period of time (12)
Trivial; silly; unimportant (9)
Unbearable (11)
Unruffled; not bothered; calmly (11)
Wasting money on extravagant purchases (11)
With disbelief (13)

87
Copyrighted

A Doll's House Vocabulary Word Search 2

Words are placed backwards, forward, diagonally, up and down. Clues listed below can help you find the words. Circle the hidden vocabulary words in the maze.

```
T K H D B I N C O M P E T E N T F S B N T
U L Z Q L L V Q G N I T A I C U R C X E R
M M D H N K U Q B C V B B E D R I D D E N
U R S S Q U A N D E R I N G Z B V Q L J M
L E U P H X R D V D L W R P V O X G J G
T F O R F N J X T E R V M R K T L H N N W
U I I N O I T U B I R T E R K S O K I H C
O N C T D K P C S J Q E D Y S Y U H S Y H
U E I E T A R E N G E E D B N N S D S P N
S M R Z E R K T P H J E J S S I S I E O R
R E P V Q V W Y P M R Q K F V R D S R C W
Z N A N S O E D C E C A Q A R E L R P R B
X T C G N E F H F R P L J Z B P V E P I J
S M M I V K I R E I B L J R D R J P U T B
D C M F V T E Z K M N E U Q R O C U S E C
S O L R X T S C I R E T S Y H A Y T W Q Q
D N D L N E F Q Y N R G A T L T H J B T Q X
J T K I H E R R N B E G A D L E P W L D K Y
A R E Y V V R X Z P X W R P L Y R M E J N L
U A V V Z C J N G M G A P R H L V A R W N P
N B A W K S U B K X C T R O M A Q C B N L K
T A S N O I T A Z I T R C J J C C M L B M
I N I Y M D S G X F M N L F V N K C B E X
L D O C Q N X S D W B M L O U S L Y W V L
Y K N P F I N C R E D U L O U S L Y W V L
```

Act of avoiding (7)
Agonizing; painful (12)
Briskly; full of self-confidence (8)
Confined to bed due to illness (9)
Costume with a hooded robe (6)
Criticism (8)
Emotional outbursts (9)
Extremely attractive (9)
Extremely noisy and disorderly (10)
Forcefully; full of strong emotions (10)
Got in the way; hindered (10)
Grabbing; taking & holding (7)
Having declined from a former state (10)
Having good manners and social graces (10)
Hold off; keep away (5)
Holding down or holding back (11)
Illegal goods (10)
Impulsive; whimsical; unpredictable (10)
Justly deserved punishment (11)
Lacking abilities (11)
Lacking discretion; not judicious; unwise (10)

Lacking respectability; shady (12)
Lively Italian dance (10)
Moved clumsily or stupidly into (9)
One who say he believes one way but whose actions show he believes the opposite (9)
Prorating or spreading the repayment of debt over a period of time (12)
Trivial; silly; unimportant (9)
Unbearable (11)
Unruffled; not bothered; calmly (11)
Wasting money on extravagant purchases (11)
With disbelief (13)

A Doll's House Vocabulary Word Search 2 Answer Key

Words are placed backwards, forward, diagonally, up and down. Clues listed below can help you find the words. Circle the hidden vocabulary words in the maze.

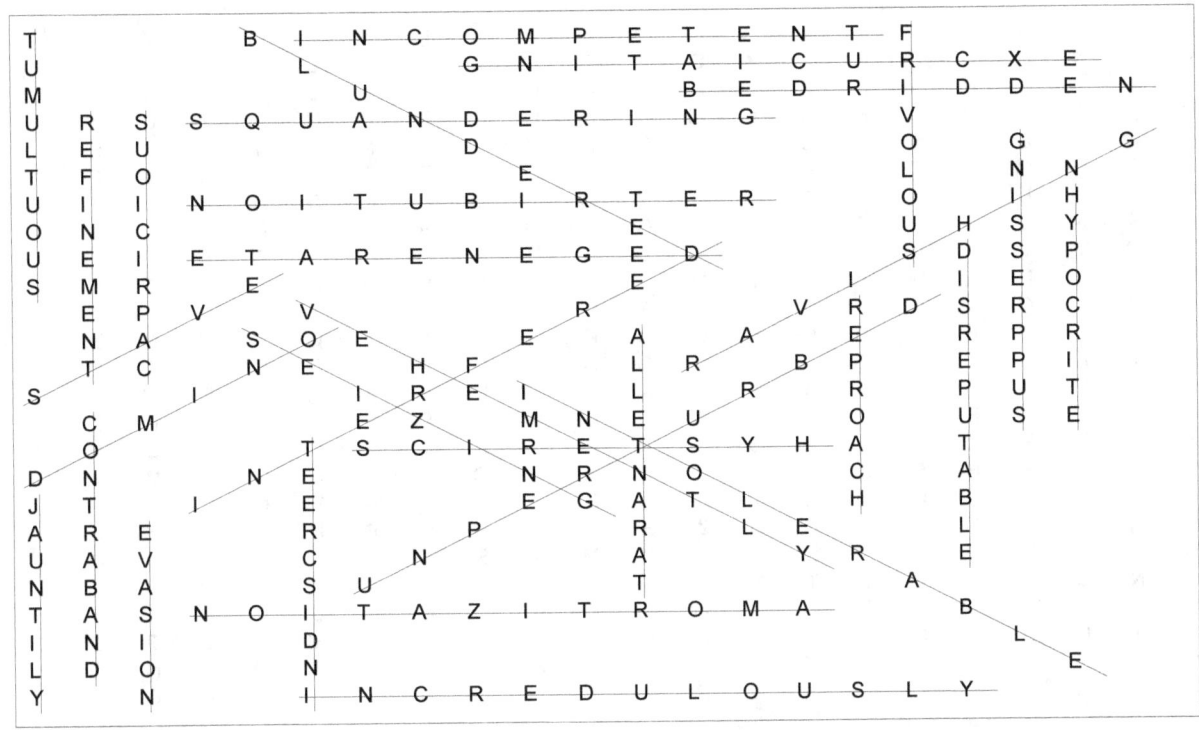

Act of avoiding (7)
Agonizing; painful (12)
Briskly; full of self-confidence (8)
Confined to bed due to illness (9)
Costume with a hooded robe (6)
Criticism (8)
Emotional outbursts (9)
Extremely attractive (9)
Extremely noisy and disorderly (10)
Forcefully; full of strong emotions (10)
Got in the way; hindered (10)
Grabbing; taking & holding (7)
Having declined from a former state (10)
Having good manners and social graces (10)
Hold off; keep away (5)
Holding down or holding back (11)
Illegal goods (10)
Impulsive; whimsical; unpredictable (10)
Justly deserved punishment (11)
Lacking abilities (11)
Lacking discretion; not judicious; unwise (10)

Lacking respectability; shady (12)
Lively Italian dance (10)
Moved clumsily or stupidly into (9)
One who say he believes one way but whose actions show he believes the opposite (9)
Prorating or spreading the repayment of debt over a period of time (12)
Trivial; silly; unimportant (9)
Unbearable (11)
Unruffled; not bothered; calmly (11)
Wasting money on extravagant purchases (11)
With disbelief (13)

A Doll's House Vocabulary Word Search 3

Words are placed backwards, forward, diagonally, up and down. Words listed below are included in the maze. Circle the hidden vocabulary words in the maze.

```
A M O R T I Z A T I O N J A U N T I L Y J
V V X I X D T X V D O E F P N B S G I E G
C X T K N V R X F I T D R Q P L Q Q N X G
D J T T V C R C T M C D I J E U L T C Z
Q C A U L R R U B D G I V F R N A V O R K
J F R M Q C B E N L G R O M T D N K L U D
Q D A U S I Q T D D R D L D U E N D H E C K
C S N L R P T L S U G E O L R R R R A Q
J N T T J V P X Z Z V V O F B E R E A P
W H E U K M Z Z V U O S Y E D I F B T H
R R L O L N T P M Y E U L D Y N I L B
Z X L U F C D F H L H R S X L G N E N W
Z M A S K H E P Z M G D E L L R E D G Z
Q L L C B T G X E H N J M E M Y R M M H
H V Z A F C E M L A V L P S S E W E R I Z
Y D X P F P N X B S T W G F W C N N S N
S D P R F B E A A E H Y P O C R I T E W W
T Q Z I Y G R G T I J D Z E L B E N L F Y
E H T C G T A C U Z R D P M V R H Y G Y Q
R D L I N Y T L P I Y M J S F A K H T C Q
I N C O M P E T E N T T E R Z R C S I D N I
C J C U W G R H R G Y Z R Z R K S I B X Y
S J L S K G C X S X N E S L S C M Y O T G
R E P R O A C H I N D O M I N O J M B N Q
S T A V E Z P H D R A V I S H I N G R G X
```

AMORTIZATION   EVASION   INTERFERED   SQUANDERING

BEDRIDDEN   EXCRUCIATING   INTOLERABLE   STAVE

BLUNDERED   FRIVOLOUS   JAUNTILY   SUPPRESSING

CAPRICIOUS   HYPOCRITE   RAVISHING   TARANTELLA

CONTRABAND   HYSTERICS   REFINEMENT   TUMULTUOUS

DEGENERATE   INCOMPETENT   REPROACH   UNPERTURBED

DISREPUTABLE   INCREDULOUSLY   RETRIBUTION   VEHEMENTLY

DOMINO   INDISCREET   SEIZING

A Doll's House Vocabulary Word Search 3 Answer Key

Words are placed backwards, forward, diagonally, up and down. Words listed below are included in the maze. Circle the hidden vocabulary words in the maze.

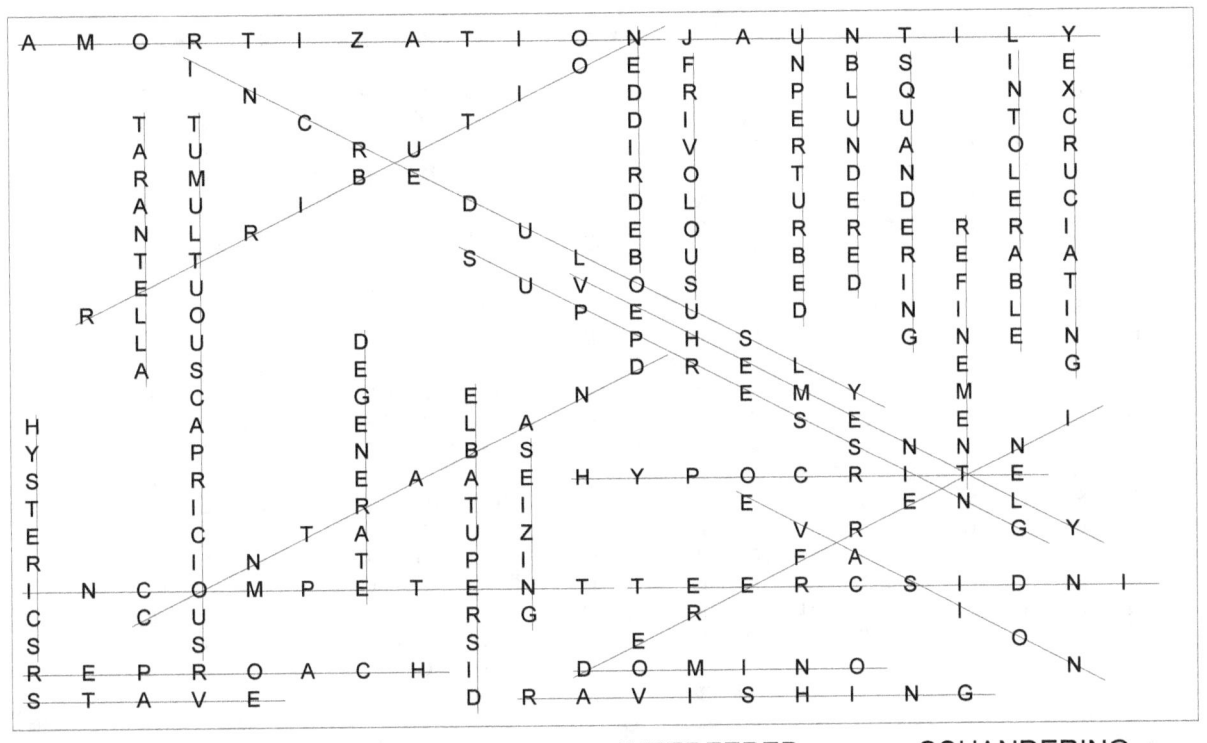

AMORTIZATION	EVASION	INTERFERED	SQUANDERING
BEDRIDDEN	EXCRUCIATING	INTOLERABLE	STAVE
BLUNDERED	FRIVOLOUS	JAUNTILY	SUPPRESSING
CAPRICIOUS	HYPOCRITE	RAVISHING	TARANTELLA
CONTRABAND	HYSTERICS	REFINEMENT	TUMULTUOUS
DEGENERATE	INCOMPETENT	REPROACH	UNPERTURBED
DISREPUTABLE	INCREDULOUSLY	RETRIBUTION	VEHEMENTLY
DOMINO	INDISCREET	SEIZING	

A Doll's House Vocabulary Word Search 4

Words are placed backwards, forward, diagonally, up and down. Words listed below are included in the maze. Circle the hidden vocabulary words in the maze.

```
F R I V O L O U S S D C N Y N O I S A V E
E T I R S C P Y H E H E O O O Y B Y B W K
X C Z B M H Y R D Z I N I P J W V D Y X
C Q A G U W R E G D K T R X T Q E M S Y X
R K B P F F B I X U W B T A R T G Z H N
U W N W R P R L B F Q V G Z P A F C V R
C L G N E I D R I V T K J V I D R B M N Y
I T I T H E C R E T K M Y G T F E W A D M
A T N R B N T I G S A Z V T R F N X D N X
T I C A U E X G O R S R P K O M E W I D D
I D R V R N K L X U E I A W M N G M S P G
N M E I B V P X F C S P N N N E Y R M H
G T D S T E P E G R Y Q R G T E D V E V D
P N U H K H W S R J N T R O L E S V P X J
Q E L I M E Z R Z T Z E K B A S C Z L U S B
Y T O N Q M N K X L U E A C J C Z L T B D X
H E U G H E R D S C I R E T S Y H A A L V
C P S M M N T H G Z E C B S L C V G B U L
L M L T U T N S K L B S D E F E C K L N F
P O Y L L L V C O Z X I F I D J D R E D X
Q C F D F Y T T X C H D Q Z N G L V Y E R
M N C Y W T N U T M K N G I M Y S G C R M
Q I L D H I F T O N Y I W N S C P N Y E R
X G N I R E D N A U Q S X G O N I M O D H
R E F I N E M E N T S J A U N T I L Y J S
```

AMORTIZATION	EVASION	INTERFERED	SQUANDERING
BEDRIDDEN	EXCRUCIATING	INTOLERABLE	STAVE
BLUNDERED	FRIVOLOUS	JAUNTILY	SUPPRESSING
CAPRICIOUS	HYPOCRITE	RAVISHING	TARANTELLA
CONTRABAND	HYSTERICS	REFINEMENT	TUMULTUOUS
DEGENERATE	INCOMPETENT	REPROACH	UNPERTURBED
DISREPUTABLE	INCREDULOUSLY	RETRIBUTION	VEHEMENTLY
DOMINO	INDISCREET	SEIZING	

A Doll's House Vocabulary Word Search 4 Answer Key

Words are placed backwards, forward, diagonally, up and down. Words listed below are included in the maze. Circle the hidden vocabulary words in the maze.

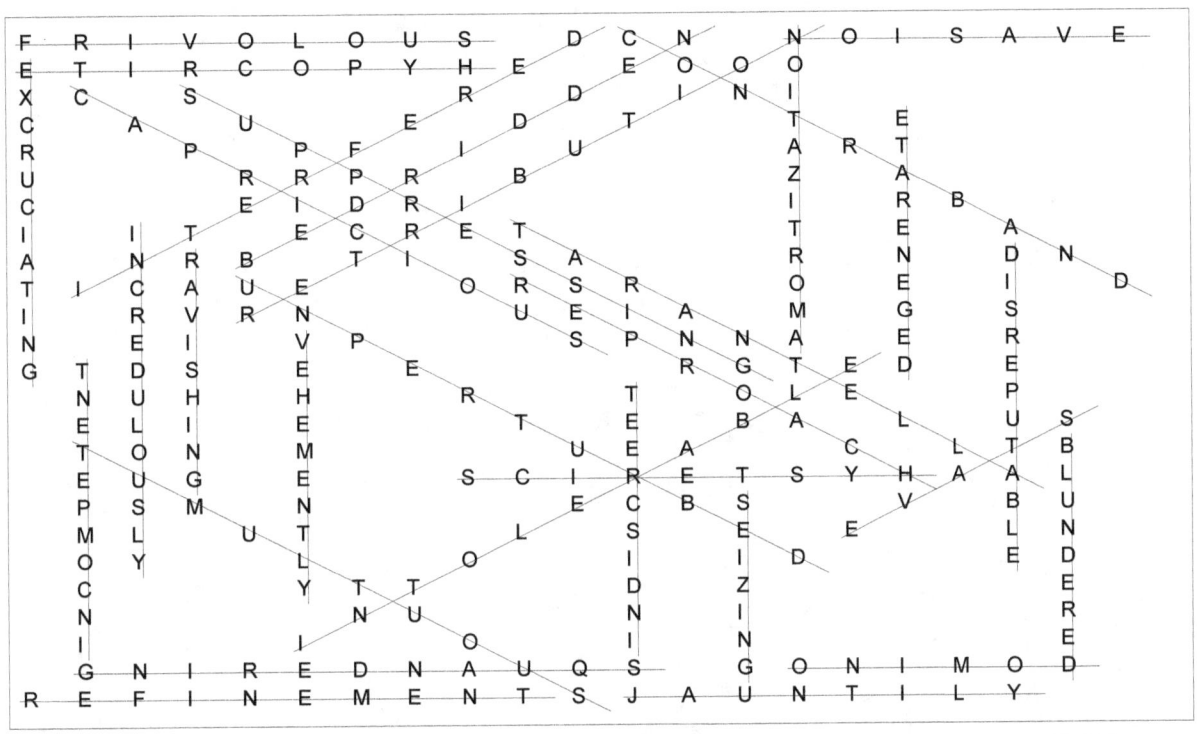

AMORTIZATION	EVASION	INTERFERED	SQUANDERING
BEDRIDDEN	EXCRUCIATING	INTOLERABLE	STAVE
BLUNDERED	FRIVOLOUS	JAUNTILY	SUPPRESSING
CAPRICIOUS	HYPOCRITE	RAVISHING	TARANTELLA
CONTRABAND	HYSTERICS	REFINEMENT	TUMULTUOUS
DEGENERATE	INCOMPETENT	REPROACH	UNPERTURBED
DISREPUTABLE	INCREDULOUSLY	RETRIBUTION	VEHEMENTLY
DOMINO	INDISCREET	SEIZING	

A Doll's House Vocabulary Crossword 1

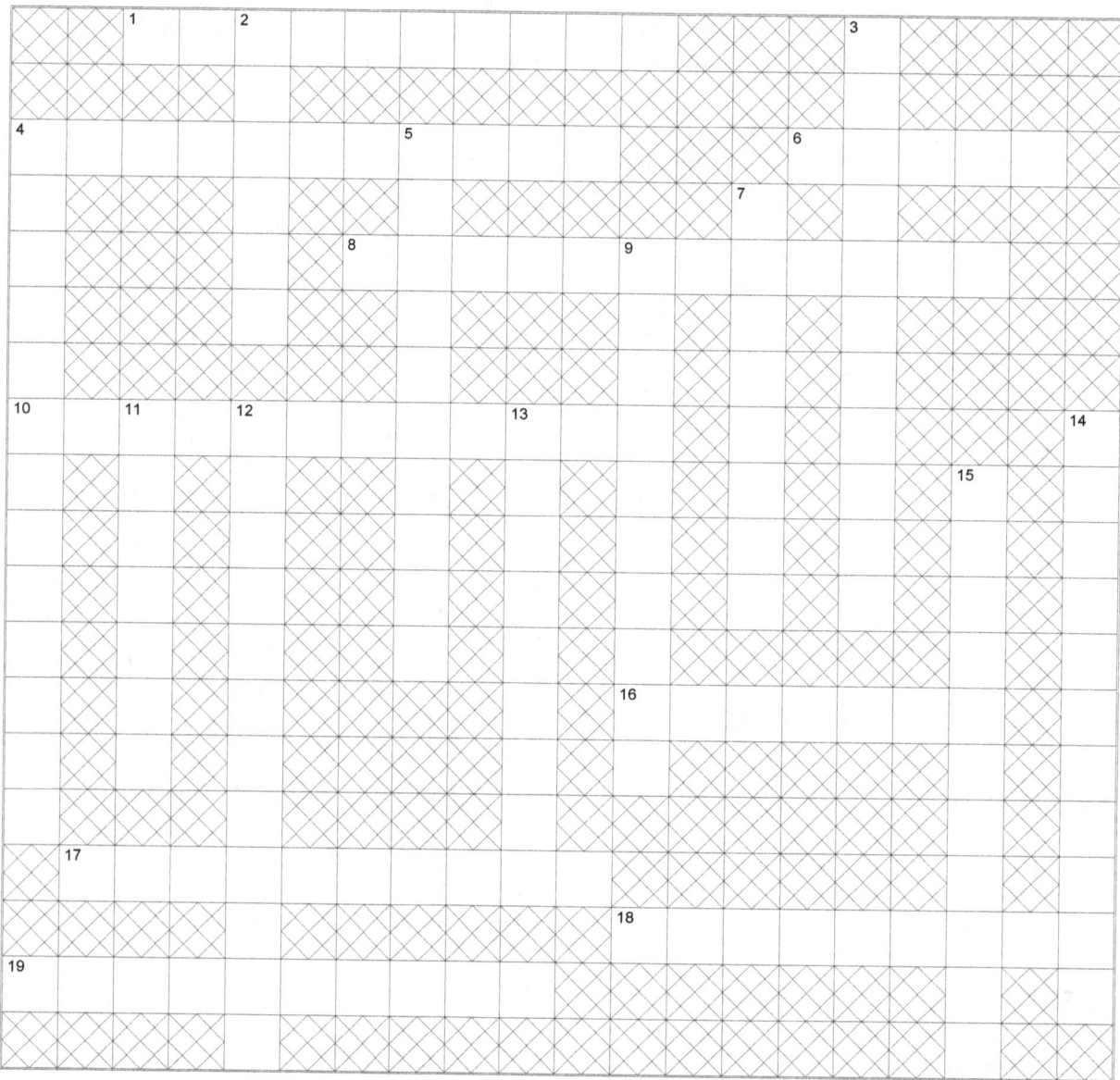

Across
1. Lacking discretion; not judicious; unwise
4. Lacking abilities
6. Hold off; keep away
8. Prorating or spreading the repayment of debt over a period of time
10. Lacking respectability; shady
16. Act of avoiding
17. Illegal goods
18. One who say he believes one way but whose actions show he believes the opposite
19. Having declined from a former state

Down
2. Costume with a hooded robe
3. Justly deserved punishment
4. With disbelief
5. Extremely noisy and disorderly
7. Briskly; full of self-confidence
9. Got in the way; hindered
11. Grabbing; taking & holding
12. Agonizing; painful
13. Confined to bed due to illness
14. Unruffled; not bothered; calmly
15. Wasting money on extravagant purchases

A Doll's House Vocabulary Crossword 1 Answer Key

		1 I	2 N	D	I	S	C	R	E	E	T		3 R		
			O										E		
4 I	N	C	O	M	5 P	E	T	E	N	T		6 S	T	A	V E
N					I				7 J		R			
C			N		8 A	M	O	R	T	I	9 Z	A	T	I	O N
R			O		U				N		U		B		
E					L				T		N		U		
10 D	11 I	12 S	R	E	P	U	T	13 A	B	L	E		T		14 U
U		E			X			U			E		I	15 S	N
L		I			C			O			D		O	Q	P
O		Z			R			U			F		N	U	E
U		I			U			S			E		Y	A	R
S		N			C			I			16 E	V	A	S	I O N	T
L		G			I			D			D			D	U
Y					A			D			D			E	R
	17 C	O	N	T	R	A	B	A	N	D				R	B
			I							18 H	Y	P	O	C	R I T E
19 D	E	G	E	N	E	R	A	T	E					N	D
			G											G	

Across
1. Lacking discretion; not judicious; unwise
4. Lacking abilities
6. Hold off; keep away
8. Prorating or spreading the repayment of debt over a period of time
10. Lacking respectability; shady
16. Act of avoiding
17. Illegal goods
18. One who say he believes one way but whose actions show he believes the opposite
19. Having declined from a former state

Down
2. Costume with a hooded robe
3. Justly deserved punishment
4. With disbelief
5. Extremely noisy and disorderly
7. Briskly; full of self-confidence
9. Got in the way; hindered
11. Grabbing; taking & holding
12. Agonizing; painful
13. Confined to bed due to illness
14. Unruffled; not bothered; calmly
15. Wasting money on extravagant purchases

A Doll's House Vocabulary Crossword 2

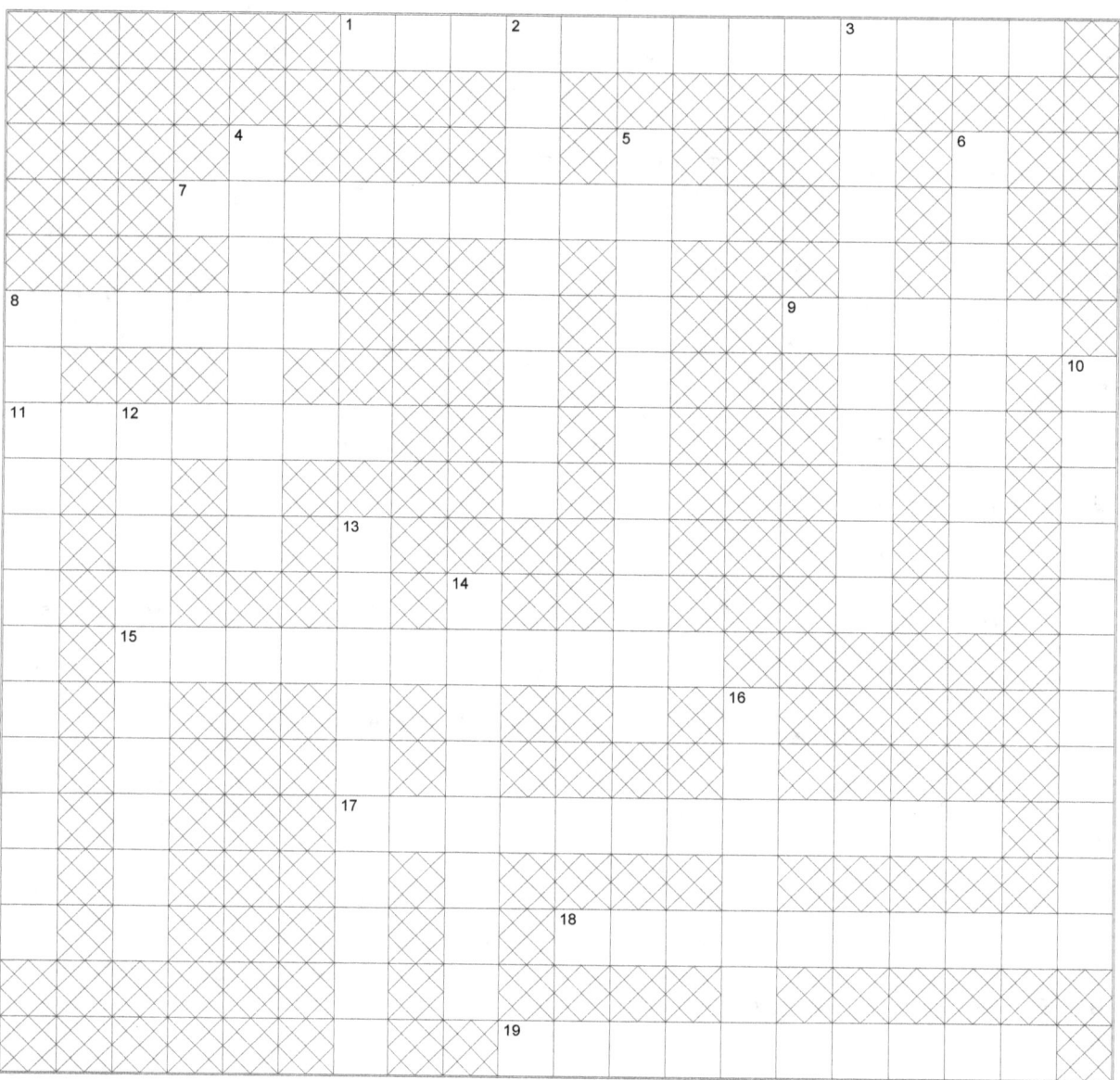

Across
1. With disbelief
7. Impulsive; whimsical; unpredictable
8. Costume with a hooded robe
9. Hold off; keep away
11. Grabbing; taking & holding
15. Wasting money on extravagant purchases
17. Prorating or spreading the repayment of debt over a period of time
18. Having good manners and social graces
19. Having declined from a former state

Down
2. Extremely attractive
3. Unruffled; not bothered; calmly
4. Briskly; full of self-confidence
5. Holding down or holding back
6. Trivial; silly; unimportant
8. Lacking respectability; shady
10. Lacking abilities
12. Lacking discretion; not judicious; unwise
13. Illegal goods
14. Criticism
16. Act of avoiding

A Doll's House Vocabulary Crossword 2 Answer Key

Across
1. With disbelief
7. Impulsive; whimsical; unpredictable
8. Costume with a hooded robe
9. Hold off; keep away
11. Grabbing; taking & holding
15. Wasting money on extravagant purchases
17. Prorating or spreading the repayment of debt over a period of time
18. Having good manners and social graces
19. Having declined from a former state

Down
2. Extremely attractive
3. Unruffled; not bothered; calmly
4. Briskly; full of self-confidence
5. Holding down or holding back
6. Trivial; silly; unimportant
8. Lacking respectability; shady
10. Lacking abilities
12. Lacking discretion; not judicious; unwise
13. Illegal goods
14. Criticism
16. Act of avoiding

A Doll's House Vocabulary Crossword 3

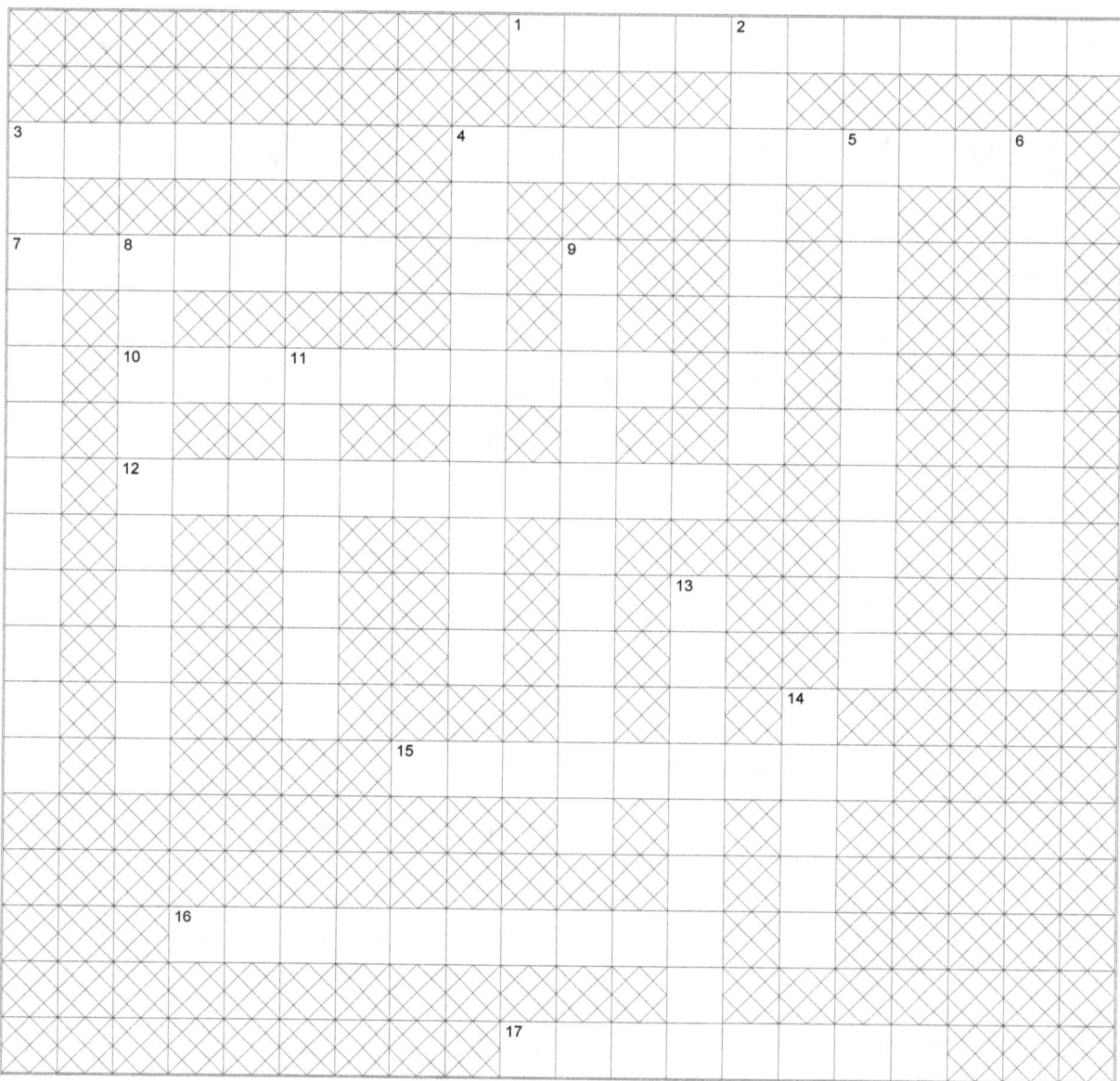

Across
1. Holding down or holding back
3. Costume with a hooded robe
4. Lacking abilities
7. Grabbing; taking & holding
10. Having declined from a former state
12. Wasting money on extravagant purchases
15. One who say he believes one way but whose actions show he believes the opposite
16. Illegal goods
17. Briskly; full of self-confidence

Down
2. Criticism
3. Lacking respectability; shady
4. Got in the way; hindered
5. Extremely noisy and disorderly
6. Lively Italian dance
8. Lacking discretion; not judicious; unwise
9. Justly deserved punishment
11. Act of avoiding
13. Confined to bed due to illness
14. Hold off; keep away

A Doll's House Vocabulary Crossword 3 Answer Key

```
                        ¹S  U  P  P  ²R  E  S  S  I  N  G
                                     E
³D  O  M  I  N  O        ⁴I  N  C  O  M  P  ⁵E  T  ⁶E  N  T
I                        N           R     U        A
⁷S  E  ⁸I  Z  I  N  G    T     ⁹R     O     M        R
R     N                  E      E     A     U        A
E     ¹⁰D  E  G  ¹¹E  N  E  R  A  T  E   C    L        N
P     I        V            F        R    H    T        T
U     ¹²S  Q  U  A  N  D  E  R  I  N  G        U        E
T     C        S            R        B         O        L
A     R        I            E     ¹³B           U        L
B     E        O            D        E         S        A
L     E        N                     D     ¹⁴S
E     T              ¹⁵H  Y  P  O  C  R  I  T  E
                         N              I     A
                         D              V
                     ¹⁶C  O  N  T  R  A  B  A  N  D  E
                                        E
                         ¹⁷J  A  U  N  T  I  L  Y
```

Across
1. Holding down or holding back
3. Costume with a hooded robe
4. Lacking abilities
7. Grabbing; taking & holding
10. Having declined from a former state
12. Wasting money on extravagant purchases
15. One who say he believes one way but whose actions show he believes the opposite
16. Illegal goods
17. Briskly; full of self-confidence

Down
2. Criticism
3. Lacking respectability; shady
4. Got in the way; hindered
5. Extremely noisy and disorderly
6. Lively Italian dance
8. Lacking discretion; not judicious; unwise
9. Justly deserved punishment
11. Act of avoiding
13. Confined to bed due to illness
14. Hold off; keep away

A Doll's House Vocabulary Crossword 4

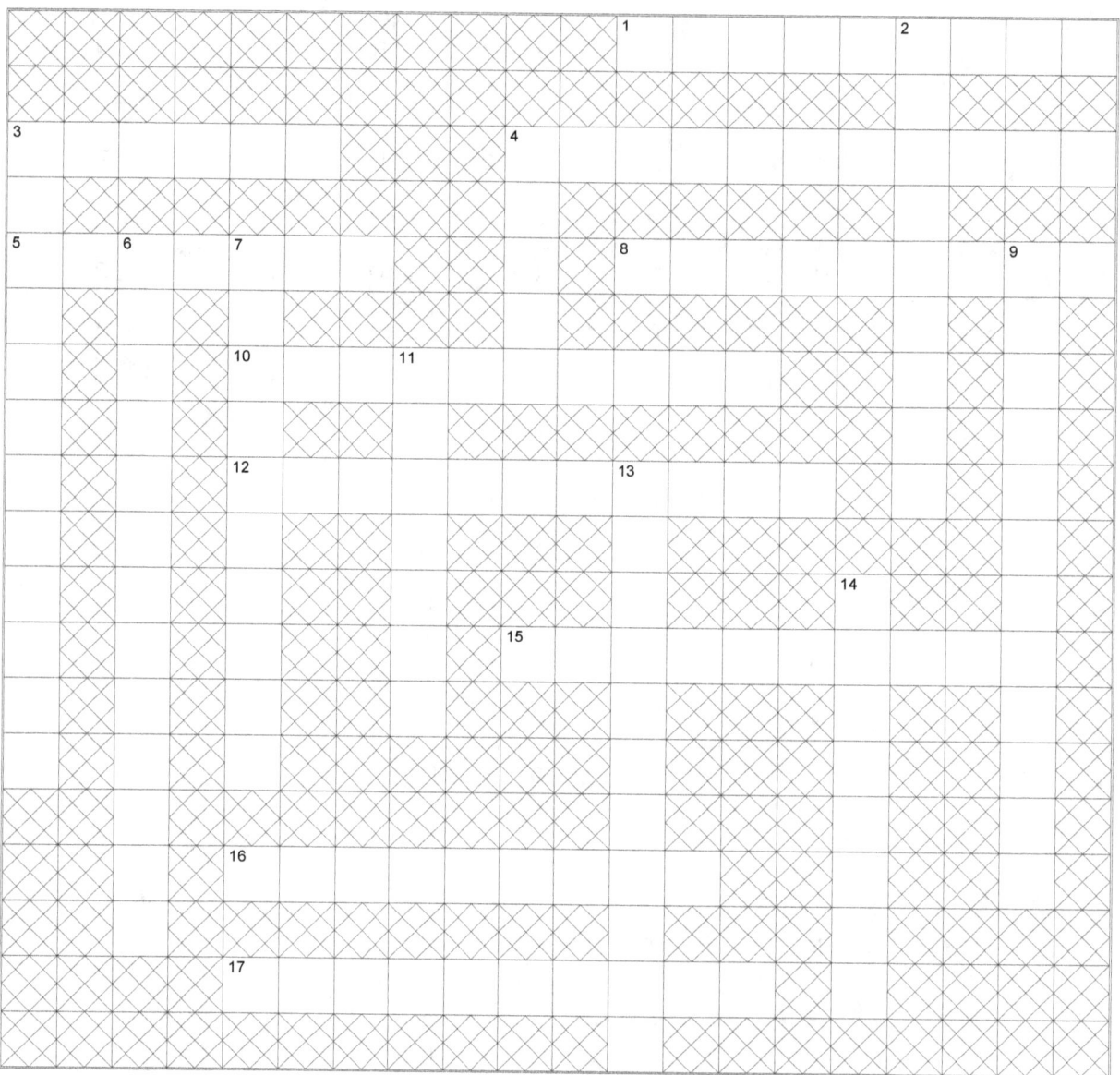

Across
1. Extremely attractive
3. Costume with a hooded robe
4. Holding down or holding back
5. Grabbing; taking & holding
8. Moved clumsily or stupidly into
10. Having declined from a former state
12. Wasting money on extravagant purchases
15. Lively Italian dance
16. One who say he believes one way but whose actions show he believes the opposite
17. Extremely noisy and disorderly

Down
2. Emotional outbursts
3. Lacking respectability; shady
4. Hold off; keep away
6. With disbelief
7. Lacking discretion; not judicious; unwise
9. Agonizing; painful
11. Act of avoiding
13. Justly deserved punishment
14. Criticism

A Doll's House Vocabulary Crossword 4 Answer Key

Across
1. Extremely attractive
3. Costume with a hooded robe
4. Holding down or holding back
5. Grabbing; taking & holding
8. Moved clumsily or stupidly into
10. Having declined from a former state
12. Wasting money on extravagant purchases
15. Lively Italian dance
16. One who say he believes one way but whose actions show he believes the opposite
17. Extremely noisy and disorderly

Down
2. Emotional outbursts
3. Lacking respectability; shady
4. Hold off; keep away
6. With disbelief
7. Lacking discretion; not judicious; unwise
9. Agonizing; painful
11. Act of avoiding
13. Justly deserved punishment
14. Criticism

A Doll's House Vocabulary Juggle Letters 1

1. SUUTOMTUUL = 1. _____
   Extremely noisy and disorderly

2. EPRRACOH = 2. _____
   Criticism

3. CMTTEEONNPI = 3. _____
   Lacking abilities

4. IOMNDO = 4. _____
   Costume with a hooded robe

5. ELRBAILOETN = 5. _____
   Unbearable

6. MNNTRIFEEE = 6. _____
   Having good manners and social graces

7. NUQERSADIGN = 7. _____
   Wasting money on extravagant purchases

8. EESBUDILRTAP = 8. _____
   Lacking respectability; shady

9. PTDENRUBREU = 9. _____
   Unruffled; not bothered; calmly

10. IISENEDCRT =10. _____
    Lacking discretion; not judicious; unwise

11. ULTANJYI =11. _____
    Briskly; full of self-confidence

12. YLCNUSUIOLRDE =12. _____
    With disbelief

13. YSHTICERS =13. _____
    Emotional outbursts

14. IDEEBDNRD =14. _____
    Confined to bed due to illness

15. HRNSIAVIG =15. _____
    Extremely attractive

A Doll's House Vocabulary Juggle Letters 1 Answer Key

1. SUUTOMTUUL = 1. TUMULTUOUS
   Extremely noisy and disorderly

2. EPRRACOH = 2. REPROACH
   Criticism

3. CMTTEEONNPI = 3. INCOMPETENT
   Lacking abilities

4. IOMNDO = 4. DOMINO
   Costume with a hooded robe

5. ELRBAILOETN = 5. INTOLERABLE
   Unbearable

6. MNNTRIFEEE = 6. REFINEMENT
   Having good manners and social graces

7. NUQERSADIGN = 7. SQUANDERING
   Wasting money on extravagant purchases

8. EESBUDILRTAP = 8. DISREPUTABLE
   Lacking respectability; shady

9. PTDENRUBREU = 9. UNPERTURBED
   Unruffled; not bothered; calmly

10. IISENEDCRT =10. INDISCREET
    Lacking discretion; not judicious; unwise

11. ULTANJYI =11. JAUNTILY
    Briskly; full of self-confidence

12. YLCNUSUIOLRDE =12. INCREDULOUSLY
    With disbelief

13. YSHTICERS =13. HYSTERICS
    Emotional outbursts

14. IDEEBDNRD =14. BEDRIDDEN
    Confined to bed due to illness

15. HRNSIAVIG =15. RAVISHING
    Extremely attractive

A Doll's House Vocabulary Juggle Letters 2

1. EYEVTHLNEM = 1. _____
   Forcefully; full of strong emotions

2. EGNISZI = 2. _____
   Grabbing; taking & holding

3. NLJIATUY = 3. _____
   Briskly; full of self-confidence

4. UPSSPRISNGE = 4. _____
   Holding down or holding back

5. GRANSIVIH = 5. _____
   Extremely attractive

6. TVESA = 6. _____
   Hold off; keep away

7. MOTITARNOZIA = 7. _____
   Prorating or spreading the repayment of debt over a period of time

8. OINBRTTURIE = 8. _____
   Justly deserved punishment

9. EIOVANS = 9. _____
   Act of avoiding

10. RASBELUIDPET =10. _____
    Lacking respectability; shady

11. XAIRCEIUTCNG =11. _____
    Agonizing; painful

12. IDOMON =12. _____
    Costume with a hooded robe

13. OEPNNIMTETC =13. _____
    Lacking abilities

14. DBNEDRIDE =14. _____
    Confined to bed due to illness

15. DNRREETFIE =15. _____
    Got in the way; hindered

A Doll's House Vocabulary Juggle Letters 2 Answer Key

1. EYEVTHLNEM = 1. VEHEMENTLY
   Forcefully; full of strong emotions

2. EGNISZI = 2. SEIZING
   Grabbing; taking & holding

3. NLJIATUY = 3. JAUNTILY
   Briskly; full of self-confidence

4. UPSSPRISNGE = 4. SUPPRESSING
   Holding down or holding back

5. GRANSIVIH = 5. RAVISHING
   Extremely attractive

6. TVESA = 6. STAVE
   Hold off; keep away

7. MOTITARNOZIA = 7. AMORTIZATION
   Prorating or spreading the repayment of debt over a period of time

8. OINBRTTURIE = 8. RETRIBUTION
   Justly deserved punishment

9. EIOVANS = 9. EVASION
   Act of avoiding

10. RASBELUIDPET = 10. DISREPUTABLE
    Lacking respectability; shady

11. XAIRCEIUTCNG = 11. EXCRUCIATING
    Agonizing; painful

12. IDOMON = 12. DOMINO
    Costume with a hooded robe

13. OEPNNIMTETC = 13. INCOMPETENT
    Lacking abilities

14. DBNEDRIDE = 14. BEDRIDDEN
    Confined to bed due to illness

15. DNRREETFIE = 15. INTERFERED
    Got in the way; hindered

A Doll's House Vocabulary Juggle Letters 3

1. UEDBNDRLE = 1. _____
   Moved clumsily or stupidly into

2. COEPHRTIY = 2. _____
   One who say he believes one way but whose actions show he believes the opposite

3. ZTAIMONIOTRA = 3. _____
   Prorating or spreading the repayment of debt over a period of time

4. NNSGERAQUDI = 4. _____
   Wasting money on extravagant purchases

5. RITETBORIUN = 5. _____
   Justly deserved punishment

6. EDIBDREDN = 6. _____
   Confined to bed due to illness

7. UUTOMTLUSU = 7. _____
   Extremely noisy and disorderly

8. TULIJYNA = 8. _____
   Briskly; full of self-confidence

9. VOIASEN = 9. _____
   Act of avoiding

10. AENEREEDTG =10. _____
    Having declined from a former state

11. UROFSLIOV =11. _____
    Trivial; silly; unimportant

12. PRCAEORH =12. _____
    Criticism

13. URUDBTPRNEE =13. _____
    Unruffled; not bothered; calmly

14. NEIOTRELLAB =14. _____
    Unbearable

15. ENATTLRALA =15. _____
    Lively Italian dance

A Doll's House Vocabulary Juggle Letters 3 Answer Key

1. UEDBNDRLE = 1. BLUNDERED
   Moved clumsily or stupidly into

2. COEPHRTIY = 2. HYPOCRITE
   One who say he believes one way but whose actions show he believes the opposite

3. ZTAIMONIOTRA = 3. AMORTIZATION
   Prorating or spreading the repayment of debt over a period of time

4. NNSGERAQUDI = 4. SQUANDERING
   Wasting money on extravagant purchases

5. RITETBORIUN = 5. RETRIBUTION
   Justly deserved punishment

6. EDIBDREDN = 6. BEDRIDDEN
   Confined to bed due to illness

7. UUTOMTLUSU = 7. TUMULTUOUS
   Extremely noisy and disorderly

8. TULIJYNA = 8. JAUNTILY
   Briskly; full of self-confidence

9. VOIASEN = 9. EVASION
   Act of avoiding

10. AENEREEDTG = 10. DEGENERATE
    Having declined from a former state

11. UROFSLIOV = 11. FRIVOLOUS
    Trivial; silly; unimportant

12. PRCAEORH = 12. REPROACH
    Criticism

13. URUDBTPRNEE = 13. UNPERTURBED
    Unruffled; not bothered; calmly

14. NEIOTRELLAB = 14. INTOLERABLE
    Unbearable

15. ENATTLRALA = 15. TARANTELLA
    Lively Italian dance

A Doll's House Vocabulary Juggle Letters 4

1. DEEEINRRTF = 1. _____
   Got in the way; hindered

2. DGNEURQSINA = 2. _____
   Wasting money on extravagant purchases

3. TTMSULUUUO = 3. _____
   Extremely noisy and disorderly

4. RYNEUCUSLDLIO = 4. _____
   With disbelief

5. PACISROIUC = 5. _____
   Impulsive; whimsical; unpredictable

6. OATRMAINOITZ = 6. _____
   Prorating or spreading the repayment of debt over a period of time

7. MELVEHYNTE = 7. _____
   Forcefully; full of strong emotions

8. LTAYIUNJ = 8. _____
   Briskly; full of self-confidence

9. CRHSIYSET = 9. _____
   Emotional outbursts

10. IFMNTNEEER = 10. _____
    Having good manners and social graces

11. ANNABTCRDO = 11. _____
    Illegal goods

12. BLAREUEDIPTS = 12. _____
    Lacking respectability; shady

13. REUEURDBTNP = 13. _____
    Unruffled; not bothered; calmly

14. MOIDNO = 14. _____
    Costume with a hooded robe

15. TENRILBELAO = 15. _____
    Unbearable

A Doll's House Vocabulary Juggle Letters 4 Answer Key

1. DEEEINRRTF = 1. INTERFERED
   Got in the way; hindered

2. DGNEURQSINA = 2. SQUANDERING
   Wasting money on extravagant purchases

3. TTMSULUUUO = 3. TUMULTUOUS
   Extremely noisy and disorderly

4. RYNEUCUSLDLIO = 4. INCREDULOUSLY
   With disbelief

5. PACISROIUC = 5. CAPRICIOUS
   Impulsive; whimsical; unpredictable

6. OATRMAINOITZ = 6. AMORTIZATION
   Prorating or spreading the repayment of debt over a period of time

7. MELVEHYNTE = 7. VEHEMENTLY
   Forcefully; full of strong emotions

8. LTAYIUNJ = 8. JAUNTILY
   Briskly; full of self-confidence

9. CRHSIYSET = 9. HYSTERICS
   Emotional outbursts

10. IFMNTNEEER = 10. REFINEMENT
    Having good manners and social graces

11. ANNABTCRDO = 11. CONTRABAND
    Illegal goods

12. BLAREUEDIPTS = 12. DISREPUTABLE
    Lacking respectability; shady

13. REUEURDBTNP = 13. UNPERTURBED
    Unruffled; not bothered; calmly

14. MOIDNO = 14. DOMINO
    Costume with a hooded robe

15. TENRILBELAO = 15. INTOLERABLE
    Unbearable

AMORTIZATION	Prorating or spreading the repayment of debt over a period of time
BEDRIDDEN	Confined to bed due to illness
BLUNDERED	Moved clumsily or stupidly into
CAPRICIOUS	Impulsive; whimsical; unpredictable
CONTRABAND	Illegal goods
DEGENERATE	Having declined from a former state

DISREPUTABLE	Lacking respectability; shady
DOMINO	Costume with a hooded robe
EVASION	Act of avoiding
EXCRUCIATING	Agonizing; painful
FRIVOLOUS	Trivial; silly; unimportant
HYPOCRITE	One who say he believes one way but whose actions show he believes the opposite

HYSTERICS	Emotional outbursts
INCOMPETENT	Lacking abilities
INCREDULOUSLY	With disbelief
INDISCREET	Lacking discretion; not judicious; unwise
INTERFERED	Got in the way; hindered
INTOLERABLE	Unbearable

JAUNTILY	Briskly; full of self-confidence
RAVISHING	Extremely attractive
REFINEMENT	Having good manners and social graces
REPROACH	Criticism
RETRIBUTION	Justly deserved punishment
SEIZING	Grabbing; taking & holding

SQUANDERING	Wasting money on extravagant purchases
STAVE	Hold off; keep away
SUPPRESSING	Holding down or holding back
TARANTELLA	Lively Italian dance
TUMULTUOUS	Extremely noisy and disorderly
UNPERTURBED	Unruffled; not bothered; calmly

VEHEMENTLY	Forcefully; full of strong emotions

A Doll's House Vocabulary

REPROACH	HYSTERICS	JAUNTILY	RAVISHING	CAPRICIOUS
CONTRABAND	AMORTIZATION	TARANTELLA	DOMINO	INTERFERED
INCREDULOUSLY	TUMULTUOUS	FREE SPACE	VEHEMENTLY	EXCRUCIATING
FRIVOLOUS	RETRIBUTION	DEGENERATE	STAVE	BEDRIDDEN
REFINEMENT	HYPOCRITE	EVASION	SEIZING	UNPERTURBED

A Doll's House Vocabulary

INDISCREET	INTOLERABLE	SUPPRESSING	BLUNDERED	INCOMPETENT
DISREPUTABLE	UNPERTURBED	SEIZING	EVASION	HYPOCRITE
REFINEMENT	BEDRIDDEN	FREE SPACE	DEGENERATE	RETRIBUTION
FRIVOLOUS	EXCRUCIATING	VEHEMENTLY	SQUANDERING	TUMULTUOUS
INCREDULOUSLY	INTERFERED	DOMINO	TARANTELLA	AMORTIZATION

A Doll's House Vocabulary

REFINEMENT	EXCRUCIATING	BEDRIDDEN	INTOLERABLE	EVASION
CAPRICIOUS	JAUNTILY	BLUNDERED	INTERFERED	RAVISHING
AMORTIZATION	VEHEMENTLY	FREE SPACE	INCREDULOUSLY	TUMULTUOUS
INDISCREET	SQUANDERING	UNPERTURBED	SUPPRESSING	INCOMPETENT
STAVE	RETRIBUTION	DISREPUTABLE	DEGENERATE	CONTRABAND

A Doll's House Vocabulary

FRIVOLOUS	HYSTERICS	DOMINO	TARANTELLA	HYPOCRITE
SEIZING	CONTRABAND	DEGENERATE	DISREPUTABLE	RETRIBUTION
STAVE	INCOMPETENT	FREE SPACE	UNPERTURBED	SQUANDERING
INDISCREET	TUMULTUOUS	INCREDULOUSLY	REPROACH	VEHEMENTLY
AMORTIZATION	RAVISHING	INTERFERED	BLUNDERED	JAUNTILY

A Doll's House Vocabulary

TARANTELLA	CAPRICIOUS	SEIZING	DEGENERATE	HYSTERICS
INCREDULOUSLY	TUMULTUOUS	EXCRUCIATING	AMORTIZATION	STAVE
EVASION	RETRIBUTION	FREE SPACE	REPROACH	SUPPRESSING
HYPOCRITE	INCOMPETENT	INTERFERED	BEDRIDDEN	DISREPUTABLE
FRIVOLOUS	JAUNTILY	INTOLERABLE	INDISCREET	SQUANDERING

A Doll's House Vocabulary

BLUNDERED	RAVISHING	DOMINO	CONTRABAND	VEHEMENTLY
REFINEMENT	SQUANDERING	INDISCREET	INTOLERABLE	JAUNTILY
FRIVOLOUS	DISREPUTABLE	FREE SPACE	INTERFERED	INCOMPETENT
HYPOCRITE	SUPPRESSING	REPROACH	UNPERTURBED	RETRIBUTION
EVASION	STAVE	AMORTIZATION	EXCRUCIATING	TUMULTUOUS

A Doll's House Vocabulary

REPROACH	JAUNTILY	REFINEMENT	DOMINO	UNPERTURBED
INTOLERABLE	DEGENERATE	RAVISHING	EVASION	HYPOCRITE
SQUANDERING	FRIVOLOUS	FREE SPACE	VEHEMENTLY	SUPPRESSING
CAPRICIOUS	BEDRIDDEN	EXCRUCIATING	HYSTERICS	DISREPUTABLE
INCOMPETENT	TUMULTUOUS	TARANTELLA	CONTRABAND	AMORTIZATION

A Doll's House Vocabulary

INTERFERED	INDISCREET	SEIZING	BLUNDERED	STAVE
RETRIBUTION	AMORTIZATION	CONTRABAND	TARANTELLA	TUMULTUOUS
INCOMPETENT	DISREPUTABLE	FREE SPACE	EXCRUCIATING	BEDRIDDEN
CAPRICIOUS	SUPPRESSING	VEHEMENTLY	INCREDULOUSLY	FRIVOLOUS
SQUANDERING	HYPOCRITE	EVASION	RAVISHING	DEGENERATE

A Doll's House Vocabulary

HYPOCRITE	EXCRUCIATING	DOMINO	RAVISHING	AMORTIZATION
INDISCREET	STAVE	JAUNTILY	VEHEMENTLY	TARANTELLA
INCOMPETENT	REPROACH	FREE SPACE	HYSTERICS	TUMULTUOUS
BLUNDERED	INTOLERABLE	SUPPRESSING	UNPERTURBED	EVASION
DISREPUTABLE	CONTRABAND	SQUANDERING	RETRIBUTION	INCREDULOUSLY

A Doll's House Vocabulary

SEIZING	FRIVOLOUS	BEDRIDDEN	INTERFERED	CAPRICIOUS
REFINEMENT	INCREDULOUSLY	RETRIBUTION	SQUANDERING	CONTRABAND
DISREPUTABLE	EVASION	FREE SPACE	SUPPRESSING	INTOLERABLE
BLUNDERED	TUMULTUOUS	HYSTERICS	DEGENERATE	REPROACH
INCOMPETENT	TARANTELLA	VEHEMENTLY	JAUNTILY	STAVE

A Doll's House Vocabulary

REPROACH	SQUANDERING	UNPERTURBED	INTOLERABLE	REFINEMENT
DOMINO	STAVE	DEGENERATE	FRIVOLOUS	HYPOCRITE
INTERFERED	TUMULTUOUS	FREE SPACE	CAPRICIOUS	DISREPUTABLE
CONTRABAND	HYSTERICS	BEDRIDDEN	INCOMPETENT	JAUNTILY
BLUNDERED	VEHEMENTLY	RAVISHING	TARANTELLA	SUPPRESSING

A Doll's House Vocabulary

EXCRUCIATING	RETRIBUTION	INDISCREET	AMORTIZATION	EVASION
INCREDULOUSLY	SUPPRESSING	TARANTELLA	RAVISHING	VEHEMENTLY
BLUNDERED	JAUNTILY	FREE SPACE	BEDRIDDEN	HYSTERICS
CONTRABAND	DISREPUTABLE	CAPRICIOUS	SEIZING	TUMULTUOUS
INTERFERED	HYPOCRITE	FRIVOLOUS	DEGENERATE	STAVE

A Doll's House Vocabulary

BLUNDERED	HYPOCRITE	SQUANDERING	FRIVOLOUS	INCREDULOUSLY
INTERFERED	DEGENERATE	JAUNTILY	UNPERTURBED	VEHEMENTLY
TUMULTUOUS	SEIZING	FREE SPACE	EVASION	EXCRUCIATING
AMORTIZATION	CONTRABAND	TARANTELLA	DISREPUTABLE	RAVISHING
BEDRIDDEN	CAPRICIOUS	DOMINO	STAVE	SUPPRESSING

A Doll's House Vocabulary

HYSTERICS	REFINEMENT	RETRIBUTION	INTOLERABLE	INCOMPETENT
REPROACH	SUPPRESSING	STAVE	DOMINO	CAPRICIOUS
BEDRIDDEN	RAVISHING	FREE SPACE	TARANTELLA	CONTRABAND
AMORTIZATION	EXCRUCIATING	EVASION	INDISCREET	SEIZING
TUMULTUOUS	VEHEMENTLY	UNPERTURBED	JAUNTILY	DEGENERATE

A Doll's House Vocabulary

INCREDULOUSLY	SQUANDERING	SEIZING	INCOMPETENT	RETRIBUTION
RAVISHING	CONTRABAND	CAPRICIOUS	REFINEMENT	INTERFERED
BEDRIDDEN	VEHEMENTLY	FREE SPACE	JAUNTILY	SUPPRESSING
TUMULTUOUS	STAVE	INTOLERABLE	EXCRUCIATING	AMORTIZATION
HYPOCRITE	EVASION	INDISCREET	FRIVOLOUS	BLUNDERED

A Doll's House Vocabulary

DEGENERATE	UNPERTURBED	TARANTELLA	REPROACH	HYSTERICS
DISREPUTABLE	BLUNDERED	FRIVOLOUS	INDISCREET	EVASION
HYPOCRITE	AMORTIZATION	FREE SPACE	INTOLERABLE	STAVE
TUMULTUOUS	SUPPRESSING	JAUNTILY	DOMINO	VEHEMENTLY
BEDRIDDEN	INTERFERED	REFINEMENT	CAPRICIOUS	CONTRABAND

A Doll's House Vocabulary

INCOMPETENT	FRIVOLOUS	INTERFERED	EVASION	EXCRUCIATING
SQUANDERING	DEGENERATE	JAUNTILY	SUPPRESSING	CAPRICIOUS
STAVE	REPROACH	FREE SPACE	INTOLERABLE	SEIZING
HYPOCRITE	CONTRABAND	BEDRIDDEN	HYSTERICS	DOMINO
RAVISHING	REFINEMENT	INDISCREET	VEHEMENTLY	UNPERTURBED

A Doll's House Vocabulary

DISREPUTABLE	RETRIBUTION	TUMULTUOUS	AMORTIZATION	TARANTELLA
BLUNDERED	UNPERTURBED	VEHEMENTLY	INDISCREET	REFINEMENT
RAVISHING	DOMINO	FREE SPACE	BEDRIDDEN	CONTRABAND
HYPOCRITE	SEIZING	INTOLERABLE	INCREDULOUSLY	REPROACH
STAVE	CAPRICIOUS	SUPPRESSING	JAUNTILY	DEGENERATE

A Doll's House Vocabulary

HYSTERICS	DOMINO	DEGENERATE	INTERFERED	BEDRIDDEN
VEHEMENTLY	JAUNTILY	INCREDULOUSLY	INCOMPETENT	INDISCREET
CAPRICIOUS	RAVISHING	FREE SPACE	EVASION	SEIZING
SQUANDERING	SUPPRESSING	AMORTIZATION	TARANTELLA	RETRIBUTION
TUMULTUOUS	DISREPUTABLE	CONTRABAND	STAVE	EXCRUCIATING

A Doll's House Vocabulary

REFINEMENT	HYPOCRITE	FRIVOLOUS	BLUNDERED	INTOLERABLE
UNPERTURBED	EXCRUCIATING	STAVE	CONTRABAND	DISREPUTABLE
TUMULTUOUS	RETRIBUTION	FREE SPACE	AMORTIZATION	SUPPRESSING
SQUANDERING	SEIZING	EVASION	REPROACH	RAVISHING
CAPRICIOUS	INDISCREET	INCOMPETENT	INCREDULOUSLY	JAUNTILY

A Doll's House Vocabulary

STAVE	UNPERTURBED	CAPRICIOUS	JAUNTILY	HYPOCRITE
RETRIBUTION	SQUANDERING	INCOMPETENT	INTERFERED	REPROACH
REFINEMENT	EXCRUCIATING	FREE SPACE	DEGENERATE	EVASION
RAVISHING	INDISCREET	HYSTERICS	DOMINO	SEIZING
BLUNDERED	INCREDULOUSLY	BEDRIDDEN	AMORTIZATION	DISREPUTABLE

A Doll's House Vocabulary

CONTRABAND	INTOLERABLE	VEHEMENTLY	SUPPRESSING	TUMULTUOUS
TARANTELLA	DISREPUTABLE	AMORTIZATION	BEDRIDDEN	INCREDULOUSLY
BLUNDERED	SEIZING	FREE SPACE	HYSTERICS	INDISCREET
RAVISHING	EVASION	DEGENERATE	FRIVOLOUS	EXCRUCIATING
REFINEMENT	REPROACH	INTERFERED	INCOMPETENT	SQUANDERING

A Doll's House Vocabulary

TUMULTUOUS	EXCRUCIATING	AMORTIZATION	FRIVOLOUS	UNPERTURBED
BEDRIDDEN	TARANTELLA	RETRIBUTION	RAVISHING	VEHEMENTLY
CONTRABAND	INDISCREET	FREE SPACE	DISREPUTABLE	HYPOCRITE
JAUNTILY	CAPRICIOUS	STAVE	INCOMPETENT	HYSTERICS
SUPPRESSING	EVASION	DOMINO	BLUNDERED	INTOLERABLE

A Doll's House Vocabulary

REFINEMENT	SQUANDERING	REPROACH	DEGENERATE	SEIZING
INCREDULOUSLY	INTOLERABLE	BLUNDERED	DOMINO	EVASION
SUPPRESSING	HYSTERICS	FREE SPACE	STAVE	CAPRICIOUS
JAUNTILY	HYPOCRITE	DISREPUTABLE	INTERFERED	INDISCREET
CONTRABAND	VEHEMENTLY	RAVISHING	RETRIBUTION	TARANTELLA

A Doll's House Vocabulary

STAVE	CAPRICIOUS	DOMINO	INTOLERABLE	UNPERTURBED
EXCRUCIATING	INCOMPETENT	REFINEMENT	INTERFERED	SQUANDERING
CONTRABAND	HYPOCRITE	FREE SPACE	BEDRIDDEN	BLUNDERED
RETRIBUTION	RAVISHING	REPROACH	SUPPRESSING	DEGENERATE
DISREPUTABLE	TUMULTUOUS	FRIVOLOUS	INDISCREET	INCREDULOUSLY

A Doll's House Vocabulary

TARANTELLA	HYSTERICS	JAUNTILY	AMORTIZATION	VEHEMENTLY
SEIZING	INCREDULOUSLY	INDISCREET	FRIVOLOUS	TUMULTUOUS
DISREPUTABLE	DEGENERATE	FREE SPACE	REPROACH	RAVISHING
RETRIBUTION	BLUNDERED	BEDRIDDEN	EVASION	HYPOCRITE
CONTRABAND	SQUANDERING	INTERFERED	REFINEMENT	INCOMPETENT

A Doll's House Vocabulary

EXCRUCIATING	SUPPRESSING	INTOLERABLE	HYPOCRITE	VEHEMENTLY
REPROACH	TARANTELLA	INDISCREET	RETRIBUTION	UNPERTURBED
SQUANDERING	INCREDULOUSLY	FREE SPACE	JAUNTILY	DOMINO
CONTRABAND	DISREPUTABLE	INTERFERED	REFINEMENT	RAVISHING
FRIVOLOUS	HYSTERICS	EVASION	INCOMPETENT	BLUNDERED

A Doll's House Vocabulary

TUMULTUOUS	STAVE	CAPRICIOUS	DEGENERATE	AMORTIZATION
BEDRIDDEN	BLUNDERED	INCOMPETENT	EVASION	HYSTERICS
FRIVOLOUS	RAVISHING	FREE SPACE	INTERFERED	DISREPUTABLE
CONTRABAND	DOMINO	JAUNTILY	SEIZING	INCREDULOUSLY
SQUANDERING	UNPERTURBED	RETRIBUTION	INDISCREET	TARANTELLA

A Doll's House Vocabulary

AMORTIZATION	INTERFERED	STAVE	INDISCREET	INCREDULOUSLY
TARANTELLA	DISREPUTABLE	JAUNTILY	REFINEMENT	REPROACH
CONTRABAND	EVASION	FREE SPACE	CAPRICIOUS	BEDRIDDEN
DOMINO	SUPPRESSING	SQUANDERING	UNPERTURBED	EXCRUCIATING
TUMULTUOUS	VEHEMENTLY	INTOLERABLE	HYSTERICS	SEIZING

A Doll's House Vocabulary

INCOMPETENT	HYPOCRITE	DEGENERATE	RAVISHING	FRIVOLOUS
RETRIBUTION	SEIZING	HYSTERICS	INTOLERABLE	VEHEMENTLY
TUMULTUOUS	EXCRUCIATING	FREE SPACE	SQUANDERING	SUPPRESSING
DOMINO	BEDRIDDEN	CAPRICIOUS	BLUNDERED	EVASION
CONTRABAND	REPROACH	REFINEMENT	JAUNTILY	DISREPUTABLE

A Doll's House Vocabulary

EVASION	TUMULTUOUS	INTOLERABLE	HYSTERICS	UNPERTURBED
INCOMPETENT	INCREDULOUSLY	SQUANDERING	BEDRIDDEN	EXCRUCIATING
DOMINO	DEGENERATE	FREE SPACE	HYPOCRITE	CAPRICIOUS
RAVISHING	INDISCREET	BLUNDERED	REPROACH	AMORTIZATION
VEHEMENTLY	STAVE	DISREPUTABLE	RETRIBUTION	FRIVOLOUS

A Doll's House Vocabulary

CONTRABAND	TARANTELLA	REFINEMENT	SEIZING	INTERFERED
JAUNTILY	FRIVOLOUS	RETRIBUTION	DISREPUTABLE	STAVE
VEHEMENTLY	AMORTIZATION	FREE SPACE	BLUNDERED	INDISCREET
RAVISHING	CAPRICIOUS	HYPOCRITE	SUPPRESSING	DEGENERATE
DOMINO	EXCRUCIATING	BEDRIDDEN	SQUANDERING	INCREDULOUSLY

www.ingramcontent.com/pod-product-compliance
Lightning Source LLC
Chambersburg PA
CBHW081458070526
44586CB00019B/2406